Simple 1-2-3™
One Dish

Publications International, Ltd.

Favorite Brand Name Recipes at www.fbnr.com

Microwave Cooking: Microwave ovens vary in wattage. Use the cooking times as guidelines and check for doneness before adding more time.

Contents

Beef in a Hurry

Zesty Italian Stuffed Peppers

3 bell peppers (green, red or yellow)
1 pound ground beef
1 jar (14 ounces) spaghetti sauce
1⅓ cups *French's*® French Fried Onions, divided
2 tablespoons *Frank's*® *RedHot*® Original Cayenne Pepper Sauce
½ cup uncooked instant rice
¼ cup sliced ripe olives
1 cup (4 ounces) shredded mozzarella cheese

Preheat oven to 400°F. Cut bell peppers in half lengthwise through stems; discard seeds. Place pepper halves, cut sides up, in shallow 2-quart baking dish; set aside.

Place beef in large microwavable bowl. Microwave on HIGH 5 minutes or until meat is browned, stirring once. Drain. Stir in spaghetti sauce, *⅔ cup* French Fried Onions, *Frank's RedHot* Sauce, rice and olives. Spoon evenly into bell pepper halves.

Cover; bake 35 minutes or until bell peppers are tender. Uncover; sprinkle with cheese and remaining *⅔ cup* onions. Bake 1 minute or until onions are golden brown.   *Makes 6 servings*

Cajun Chili

1½ pounds ground beef
2 cans (15 ounces each) Cajun-style mixed vegetables, undrained
2 cans (10¾ ounces each) condensed tomato soup, undiluted
1 can (about 14 ounces) diced tomatoes
3 sausages with Cheddar cheese (about 8 ounces), cut into bite-size pieces
Shredded Cheddar cheese

Slow Cooker Directions

1. Brown beef in large nonstick skillet over medium-high heat, stirring to break up meat. Drain fat.

2. Place beef, mixed vegetables with juice, soup, tomatoes and sausages in slow cooker.

3. Cover; cook on HIGH 2 to 3 hours. Serve with cheese.

Makes 10 servings

Cajun-Style Mixed Vegetables

Tomato Soup

Beef in a Hurry

Hearty Ground Beef Stew

1. Brown beef with garlic in large saucepan; drain. Add remaining ingredients. Heat to boiling. Cover. Reduce heat to medium-low. Cook 10 minutes or until vegetables are crisp-tender.

2. Serve in warm bowls with garlic bread, if desired.   *Makes 6 servings*

1 pound ground beef
3 cloves garlic, minced
1 package (16 ounces)
    Italian-style frozen
    vegetables
2 cups southern-style hash
    brown potatoes
1 jar (14 ounces) marinara
    sauce
1 can (10½ ounces)
    condensed beef broth,
    undiluted
3 tablespoons *French's®*
    Worcestershire Sauce

Beef in a Hurry

1 tablespoon vegetable oil
1 small onion, chopped
1 pound ground beef chuck
1 package (about 1 ounce) taco seasoning mix
1 can (8 ounces) tomato sauce
¼ cup raisins
2 teaspoons dark brown sugar
1 package (8 count) refrigerated crescent rolls
Sliced green onion (optional)

Empanada Pie

1. Preheat oven to 375°F. Grease 10-inch shallow round baking dish or deep-dish pie plate.

2. Heat oil in large skillet over medium-high heat. Add onion; cook 2 to 3 minutes or until translucent. Add ground beef. Brown beef, stirring to break up meat. Drain fat. Sprinkle taco mix over beef mixture. Add tomato sauce, raisins and sugar. Reduce heat to low; cook 2 to 3 minutes.

3. Spoon beef mixture into prepared dish. Unroll crescent dough; divide into triangles. Arrange in spiral with points of dough towards center. Do not seal dough pieces together.

4. Bake 13 to 17 minutes or until dough is puffed and golden brown. Garnish with green onion.

Makes 4 to 6 servings

Beef in a Hurry

Stuffed Mexican Pizza Pie

1. Preheat oven to 425°F. Spray 13×9-inch baking pan with cooking spray; set aside.

2. Spray large nonstick skillet with nonstick cooking spray; heat over high heat until hot. Add beef, onion and bell pepper; cook and stir 5 minutes or until meat is no longer pink.

3. Add rice, stewed tomatoes and water. Bring to a boil. Pour beef mixture into prepared baking pan. Sprinkle with 1¼ cups cheese and stir until blended.

4. Unroll pizza crust dough on work surface. Place dough in one even layer over mixture in baking pan. Cut 6 to 8 slits in dough with sharp knife. Bake 10 minutes or until crust is lightly browned. Sprinkle top of crust with remaining ¾ cup cheese; continue baking 4 minutes or until cheese is melted and crust is deep golden brown.

5. Let stand 5 minutes before cutting. *Makes 6 servings*

1 pound ground beef
1 large onion, chopped
1 large green bell pepper, chopped
1½ cups UNCLE BEN'S® Instant Rice
2 cans (14½ ounces each) Mexican-style stewed tomatoes, undrained
⅔ cup water
2 cups (8 ounces) shredded Mexican-style seasoned Monterey Jack-Colby cheese blend, divided
1 package (10 ounces) refrigerated pizza crust dough

Beef in a Hurry

Mushroom-Beef Stew

1 pound beef for stew
1 can (10¾ ounces)
    condensed cream of
    mushroom soup,
    undiluted
2 cans (4 ounces each)
    sliced mushrooms,
    drained
1 package (1 ounce) dry
    onion soup mix
    Hot cooked noodles

Slow Cooker Directions

Combine all ingredients except noodles in slow cooker. Cover; cook on LOW 8 to 10 hours. Serve over noodles.   *Makes 4 servings*

Beef in a Hurry

Quick 'n' Tangy Beef Stir-Fry

1. Combine ingredients for sauce. Marinate beef in ¼ *cup* sauce 5 minutes. Heat *1 tablespoon oil* in large skillet or wok over high heat. Stir-fry beef in batches 5 minutes or until browned.

2. Add peppers; cook 2 minutes. Add remaining sauce; stir-fry until sauce thickens. Serve over hot cooked ramen noodles or rice, if desired.

Makes 4 servings

Sauce

- ½ **cup** *French's®* **Worcestershire Sauce**
- ½ **cup water**
- 2 **tablespoons sugar**
- 2 **teaspoons cornstarch**
- ½ **teaspoon ground ginger**
- ½ **teaspoon garlic powder**

Stir-fry

- 1 **pound thinly sliced beef steak**
- 3 **cups sliced bell peppers**

Biscuit-Topped Hearty Steak Pie

1½ pounds top round steak, cooked and cut into 1-inch cubes

1 package (9 ounces) frozen baby carrots

1 package (9 ounces) frozen peas and pearl onions

1 large baking potato, baked and cut into ½-inch pieces

1 jar (18 ounces) home-style brown gravy

½ teaspoon dried thyme

½ teaspoon black pepper

1 can (10 ounces) refrigerated flaky buttermilk biscuits

1. Preheat oven to 375°F. Spray 2-quart casserole with nonstick cooking spray.

2. Combine steak, frozen vegetables and potato in prepared dish. Stir in gravy, thyme and pepper.

3. Bake, uncovered, 40 minutes. Remove from oven. *Increase oven temperature to 400°F.* Top with biscuits and bake 8 to 10 minutes or until biscuits are golden brown. *Makes 6 servings*

Tip: This casserole can be prepared with leftovers of almost any kind. Other steaks, roast beef, stew meat, pork, lamb or chicken can be substituted for the round steak; adjust the gravy flavor to complement the meat. Red potatoes can be used in place of the baking potato. Choose your favorite vegetable combination, such as broccoli, cauliflower and carrots, or broccoli, corn and red peppers, as a substitute for the peas and carrots.

Chuckwagon BBQ Rice Round-Up

1. In large skillet over medium-high heat, brown ground beef until well cooked. Remove from skillet; drain. Set aside.

2. In same skillet over medium heat, sauté rice-vermicelli mix with margarine until vermicelli is golden brown.

3. Slowly stir in 2½ cups water, corn and Special Seasonings; bring to a boil. Reduce heat to low. Cover; simmer 15 to 20 minutes or until rice is tender.

4. Stir in barbecue sauce and ground beef. Sprinkle with cheese. Cover; let stand 3 to 5 minutes or until cheese is melted.   *Makes 4 servings*

Tip: Salsa can be substituted for barbecue sauce.

1 **pound lean ground beef**
1 **(6.8-ounce) package RICE-A-RONI® Beef Flavor**
2 **tablespoons margarine or butter**
2 **cups frozen corn**
½ **cup prepared barbecue sauce**
½ **cup (2 ounces) shredded Cheddar cheese**

Beef in a Hurry

Tamale Beef Squares

1 (6½-ounce) package
  corn muffin and
  cornbread mix
⅓ cup milk
¼ cup cholesterol-free egg
  substitute
1 tablespoon oil
1 pound ground beef
¾ cup chopped onion
1 cup frozen corn kernels
1 can (about 14 ounces)
  Mexican-style stewed
  tomatoes
2 teaspoons cornstarch
¾ cup shredded sharp
  Cheddar cheese
  (3 ounces)

1. Preheat oven to 400°F. Spray 12×8-inch baking dish with nonstick cooking spray.

2. Stir together corn muffin mix, milk, egg substitute and oil. Spread in bottom of prepared dish.

3. Cook ground beef and onion in large skillet over medium-high heat until beef is lightly browned, stirring to break up meat; drain fat. Stir in corn.

4. Mix together tomatoes and cornstarch, breaking up any large pieces of tomato. Stir into beef mixture. Bring to a boil, stirring frequently.

5. Spoon beef mixture over cornbread mixture. Cover with foil. Bake 15 minutes. Uncover; bake 10 minutes more. Sprinkle with cheese. Return to oven; bake 2 to 3 minutes or until cheese melts. Let stand 5 minutes. Cut into squares. *Makes 6 servings*

Beef in a Hurry

Oven-Baked Stew

1. Preheat oven to 425°F. In 2½-quart shallow casserole, toss beef with flour, then bake uncovered 20 minutes, stirring once.

2. *Reduce heat to 350°F.* Stir in carrots, tomatoes, soup mix and wine.

3. Bake covered 1½ hours or until beef is tender. Stir in mushrooms and bake covered an additional 10 minutes. Serve over hot noodles.

Makes 8 servings

Slow Cooker Method: In slow cooker, toss beef with flour. Add carrots, tomatoes, soup mix and wine. Cook covered on LOW 8 to 10 hours. Add mushrooms; cook covered on LOW 30 minutes or until beef is tender. Serve over hot noodles.

2 pounds boneless beef chuck steak, cut into 1-inch cubes
¼ cup all-purpose flour
1⅓ cups sliced carrots
1 can (about 14 ounces) diced tomatoes, undrained
1 envelope LIPTON® RECIPE SECRETS® Onion Soup Mix*
½ cup dry red wine or water
1 cup sliced mushrooms
1 package (8 ounces) egg noodles, cooked and drained

*Also terrific with LIPTON® RECIPE SECRETS® Beefy Onion, Onion Mushroom or Beefy Mushroom Soup Mix.

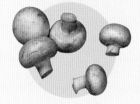

Tortilla Beef Casserole

1 package (about 17 ounces) refrigerated fully cooked beef pot roast in gravy*

6 (6-inch) corn tortillas, cut into 1-inch pieces

1 jar (16 ounces) salsa

1½ cups canned or frozen corn kernels

1 cup black or pinto beans, rinsed and drained

1 cup (8 ounces) Mexican cheese blend

Fully cooked beef roast can be found in the refrigerated prepared meats section of the supermarket.

1. Preheat oven to 350°F. Lightly spray 11×7-inch casserole or 2-quart casserole with nonstick cooking spray.

2. Drain and discard gravy from beef. Cut or shred beef into bite-size pieces.

3. Combine beef, tortillas, salsa, corn and beans in large bowl; mix well. Transfer to prepared casserole. Bake 20 minutes or until heated through. Top with cheese; bake 5 minutes more or until cheese is melted.

Makes 4 servings

Beef in a Hurry

Beef & Broccoli Pepper Steak

1. In large skillet over medium-high heat, melt 1 tablespoon margarine. Add steak; sauté 3 minutes or until just browned. Remove from skillet; set aside.

2. In same skillet over medium heat, sauté rice-vermicelli mix with remaining 2 tablespoons margarine until vermicelli is golden brown. Slowly stir in 2½ cups water and Special Seasonings; bring to a boil. Reduce heat to low. Cover; simmer 10 minutes.

3. Stir in steak, broccoli, bell pepper and onion; return to a simmer. Cover; simmer 5 to 10 minutes or until rice is tender.   *Makes 4 servings*

- 3 tablespoons margarine or butter, divided
- 1 pound sirloin or top round steak, cut into thin strips
- 1 (6.8-ounce) package RICE-A-RONI® Beef Flavor
- 2 cups broccoli flowerets
- ½ cup red or green bell pepper strips
- 1 small onion, thinly sliced

Beef in a Hurry

Spaghetti Rolls

1 package (8 ounces)
   manicotti shells
2 pounds ground beef
1 tablespoon onion powder
1 teaspoon salt
½ teaspoon black pepper
2 cups pasta sauce, divided
1 cup (4 ounces) shredded
   pizza cheese blend or
   mozzarella cheese

1. Cook pasta according to package directions. Drain in colander, then rinse under warm running water. Drain well.

2. Preheat oven to 350°F. Grease 13×9-inch baking pan.

3. Brown beef in large skillet over medium-high heat, stirring to break up meat; drain fat. Stir in onion powder, salt and pepper. Stir in 1 cup pasta sauce; cool and set aside.

4. Reserve ½ cup ground beef mixture. Combine remaining beef mixture with cheese in large bowl; fill shells with beef mixture using spoon.

5. Arrange shells in prepared pan. Combine remaining 1 cup pasta sauce and reserved beef mixture in small bowl; blend well. Pour over shells. Cover with foil.

6. Bake 20 to 30 minutes or until hot.

Makes 4 servings

Beef in a Hurry

Mexican Beef Stir-Fry

Cut steak across the grain into ⅛-inch-thick strips. Combine oil, cumin, oregano and garlic in small bowl. Heat ½ oil mixture in large nonstick skillet over medium-high heat. Add bell pepper, onion and jalapeño pepper; stir-fry 2 to 3 minutes or until crisp-tender. Remove and reserve. In same skillet, stir-fry beef strips (½ at a time) in remaining oil mixture 1 to 2 minutes. Return vegetables to skillet and heat through. Serve beef mixture over lettuce.

Makes 4 servings

Tip: Recipe may also be prepared using beef top sirloin steak.

Favorite recipe from **North Dakota Beef Commission**

1 pound beef flank steak
2 tablespoons vegetable oil
1 teaspoon ground cumin
1 teaspoon dried oregano
1 clove garlic, crushed
1 red or green bell pepper, cut into thin strips
1 medium onion, cut into thin wedges
1 to 2 jalapeño peppers,* thinly sliced
3 cups thinly sliced lettuce

*Remove interior ribs and seeds if a milder flavor is desired. Jalapeño peppers can sting and irritate the skin; wear rubber gloves when handling peppers and do not touch eyes. Wash hands after handling.

Beef in a Hurry

Texas Beef Stew

1 pound lean ground beef
1 small onion, chopped
1 can (28 ounces) crushed tomatoes with roasted garlic
1½ cups BIRDS EYE® frozen Broccoli, Cauliflower & Carrots
1 can (14½ ounces) whole new potatoes, halved
1 cup BIRDS EYE® frozen Sweet Corn
1 can (4½ ounces) chopped green chilies, drained
½ cup water

• In large saucepan, cook beef and onion over medium-high heat until beef is well browned, stirring occasionally.

• Stir in tomatoes, vegetables, potatoes with liquid, corn, chilies and water; bring to a boil.

• Reduce heat to medium-low; cover and simmer 5 minutes or until heated through.   *Makes 4 servings*

Serving Suggestion: Serve over rice with warm crusty bread.

Birds Eye® Idea: The smell of onions and garlic can penetrate into your cutting boards. Keep a separate cutting board exclusively for these vegetables.

Beef in a Hurry

Pizza Pie Meatloaf

1. Preheat oven to 350°F. Combine beef, ½ *cup* mozzarella, bread crumbs, ½ *cup* tomato sauce, Parmesan cheese, Worcestershire and oregano in large bowl; stir with fork until well blended.

2. Place meat mixture into round pizza pan with edge or pie plate and shape into 9×1-inch round. Bake 35 minutes or until no longer pink in center and internal temperature reads 160°F. Drain fat.

3. Top with remaining tomato sauce, sliced tomato, green bell pepper strips, mozzarella cheese and French Fried Onions. Bake 5 minutes or until cheese is melted and onions are golden. Cut into wedges to serve.

Makes 6 to 8 servings

2 pounds ground beef
1½ cups shredded mozzarella cheese, divided
½ cup unseasoned dry breadcrumbs
1 cup tomato sauce, divided
¼ cup grated Parmesan cheese
¼ cup *French's®* Worcestershire Sauce
1 tablespoon dried oregano leaves
1 plum tomato, thinly sliced
½ cup sliced green bell pepper
1⅓ cups *French's®* French Fried Onions

Beef in a Hurry

Easy Family Burritos

1 boneless beef chuck
    shoulder roast (2 to
    3 pounds)
1 jar (24 ounces) *or* 2 jars
    (16 ounces each) salsa
Flour tortillas

Slow Cooker Directions

1. Place roast in slow cooker; top with salsa. Cover; cook on LOW 8 to 10 hours.

2. Remove beef from slow cooker. Shred meat with 2 forks. Return to slow cooker. Cover; cook on LOW 1 to 2 hours or until heated through.

3. Serve shredded meat wrapped in warm tortillas.   *Makes 8 servings*

Slow Cooker Mesquite Beef

Slow Cooker Directions

Trim fat from meat. Place meat in slow cooker. Pour ¾ cup Mesquite Marinade over meat. Cover and cook on LOW for 9 to 10 hours. Remove meat to platter and shred with fork. Return meat to slow cooker with juices; add remaining ¼ cup Mesquite Marinade. Serve shredded beef in warmed French rolls or in warmed flour tortillas or taco shells, if desired.

Makes 8 to 10 servings (or two meals of 4 to 5 servings each)

Meal Idea: Add your favorite frozen stew vegetables during the last hour of cooking for a pot roast/stew meal.

1 boneless beef chuck roast (about 4 to 5 pounds)
1 cup LAWRY'S® Mesquite Marinade with Lime Juice, divided
French rolls, flour tortillas or taco shells (optional)

Beef in a Hurry

Mexican Lasagna

1 jar (1 pound 10 ounces)
RAGÚ® Old World
Style® Pasta Sauce
1 pound ground beef
1 can (15¼ ounces) whole
kernel corn, drained
4½ teaspoons chili powder
6 (8½-inch) flour tortillas
2 cups shredded Cheddar
cheese (about
8 ounces)

1. Preheat oven to 350°F. Set aside 1 cup Ragú Pasta Sauce. In 10-inch skillet, brown ground beef over medium-high heat; drain. Stir in remaining Ragú Pasta Sauce, corn and chili powder.

2. In 13×9-inch baking dish, spread 1 cup sauce mixture. Arrange two tortillas over sauce, overlapping edges slightly. Layer half the sauce mixture and ⅓ of the cheese over tortillas; repeat layers, ending with tortillas. Spread tortillas with reserved sauce.

3. Bake 30 minutes, then top with remaining cheese and bake an additional 10 minutes or until sauce is bubbling and cheese is melted.

Makes 8 servings

Tip: Substitute refried beans for ground beef for a meatless main dish.

Beef in a Hurry

Beef and Broccoli

1. Cut beef crosswise into ⅛-inch-thick slices. Toss beef with ginger and garlic in medium bowl.

2. Heat oil in wok or large nonstick skillet over medium heat. Add half of beef mixture; stir-fry 2 to 3 minutes or until beef is barely pink in center. Remove. Repeat with remaining beef. Remove and reserve.

3. Add broccoli and water to wok; cover and steam 3 to 5 minutes or until broccoli is crisp-tender.

4. Return beef and any accumulated juices to wok. Add teriyaki sauce. Cook until heated through. Serve over rice.

Makes 4 servings

1 pound beef tenderloin steaks
2 teaspoons minced fresh ginger
2 cloves garlic, minced
½ teaspoon vegetable oil
3 cups broccoli florets
¼ cup water
2 tablespoons bottled teriyaki sauce
2 cups hot cooked white rice

Stir-Fry Beef & Vegetable Soup

1. Slice beef lengthwise in half, then crosswise into ⅛-inch-thick strips.

2. Heat Dutch oven over medium-high heat. Add 1 teaspoon sesame oil; tilt pan to coat bottom. Add half the beef in single layer; cook 1 minute, without stirring, until lightly browned on bottom. Turn; brown other side about 1 minute. Remove beef from pan; set aside. Repeat with remaining 1 teaspoon sesame oil and beef; set aside.

3. Add broth to Dutch oven. Cover; bring to a boil over high heat. Add vegetables. Reduce heat; simmer 3 to 5 minutes or until vegetables are heated through. Add beef, green onions and stir-fry sauce; simmer 1 minute.

Makes 6 servings

Serving Suggestion: Make a quick sesame bread to serve with soup. Brush refrigerated dinner roll dough with water, then dip in sesame seeds before baking.

1 boneless beef top sirloin or top round steak (about 1 pound)

2 teaspoons dark sesame oil, divided

3 cans (about 14 ounces each) beef broth

1 package (16 ounces) frozen stir-fry vegetables

3 green onions, thinly sliced

¼ cup stir-fry sauce

Main-Dish Pie

• Unroll crescent dough and separate rolls. Spread to cover bottom of ungreased 9-inch pie pan. Press together to form crust. Bake in preheated 350°F oven for 10 minutes.

• In large skillet, brown ground beef and onion; drain excess fat.

• Stir in gravy and peas; cook until heated through.

• Pour mixture into partially baked crust. Sprinkle with cheese.

• Bake 10 to 15 minutes or until crust is brown and cheese is melted.

• Arrange tomato slices over pie; bake 2 minutes more.

Makes 6 servings

1 package (8 rolls) refrigerated crescent rolls
1 pound lean ground beef
1 medium onion, chopped
1 can (12 ounces) beef or mushroom gravy
1 box (10 ounces) BIRDS EYE® frozen Green Peas, thawed
½ cup shredded Swiss cheese
5 slices tomato

Mexican-Style Shredded Beef

1 boneless beef chuck
   shoulder roast (about
   3 pounds)
1 tablespoon ground cumin
1 tablespoon ground
   coriander
1 tablespoon chili powder
1 teaspoon salt
½ teaspoon ground red
   pepper
1 cup salsa or picante
   sauce
2 tablespoons water
1 tablespoon cornstarch
   Taco shells

Slow Cooker Directions

1. Cut roast in half. Combine cumin, coriander, chili powder, salt and red pepper in small bowl. Rub over beef. Place ¼ cup salsa in slow cooker; top with one piece beef. Layer ¼ cup salsa, remaining beef and ½ cup salsa in slow cooker. Cover; cook on LOW 8 to 10 hours or until meat is tender.

2. Remove beef from cooking liquid; cool slightly. Trim and discard excess fat from beef. Shred meat with two forks.

3. Let cooking liquid stand 5 minutes to allow fat to rise. Skim off fat. Blend water and cornstarch until smooth. Whisk into liquid in slow cooker. Cook, uncovered, 15 minutes on HIGH until thickened. Return beef to slow cooker. Cover; cook 15 to 30 minutes or until hot. Adjust seasonings. Serve as meat filling for tacos, fajitas or burritos. Leftover beef may be refrigerated up to 3 days or frozen up to 3 months. *Makes 5 cups filling*

Beef in a Hurry

Beef Teriyaki Stir-Fry

1. Cook rice according to package directions.

2. Cut beef lengthwise in half, then crosswise into ⅛-inch-thick slices. Combine beef and ¼ cup marinade in medium bowl; set aside.

3. Heat 1½ teaspoons oil in wok or large skillet over medium-high heat until hot. Add onion; stir-fry 3 to 4 minutes or until crisp-tender. Remove from wok to medium bowl.

4. Heat 1½ teaspoons oil in wok. Stir-fry beans 3 minutes or until crisp-tender and hot. Drain off excess liquid. Add beans to onions in bowl.

5. Heat 1½ teaspoons oil in wok. Drain beef, discarding marinade. Stir-fry half of beef 2 minutes or until barely pink in center. Remove to bowl. Repeat with remaining oil and beef. Return beef and accumulated juices in bowl to wok. Stir in vegetables and remaining ¼ cup marinade. Cook and stir 1 minute or until heated through. Serve with rice. *Makes 4 servings*

1 cup uncooked rice
1 boneless beef top sirloin steak (about 1 pound)
½ cup teriyaki marinade and sauce, divided
2 tablespoons vegetable oil, divided
1 medium onion, halved and sliced
2 cups frozen green beans, thawed

Beef in a Hurry

Hearty Beef and Potato Casserole

1 package (about 17 ounces) refrigerated fully cooked beef pot roast in gravy*

3 cups frozen hash brown potatoes, divided

¼ teaspoon salt

¼ teaspoon black pepper

1 can (about 14 ounces) diced tomatoes, well drained

½ cup canned chipotle chile sauce

1 cup (4 ounces) shredded sharp Cheddar cheese

Fully cooked beef roast can be found in the refrigerated prepared meats section of the supermarket.

1. Preheat oven to 375°F. Grease 11×7-inch glass baking dish.

2. Drain and discard gravy from pot roast. Cut beef into ¼-inch thick slices; set aside. Place 2 cups potatoes in prepared baking dish. Sprinkle with salt and pepper. Top with beef. Combine tomatoes and chipotle sauce in small bowl; spread evenly over beef. Top with remaining potatoes. Sprinkle with cheddar cheese.

3. Lightly cover dish with foil. Bake 20 minutes. Remove foil; bake 20 minutes longer or until hot and bubbly. Let stand 5 to 10 minutes before serving.

Makes 6 servings

Beef in a Hurry

Tamale Pie

1. Preheat oven to 400°F.

2. In 12-inch skillet, heat oil over medium heat and cook onion, stirring occasionally, 3 minutes or until tender. Stir in ground beef and cook until browned.

3. Stir in onion soup mix blended with tomatoes and water. Bring to a boil over high heat, stirring with spoon to crush tomatoes. Reduce heat to low and stir in beans. Simmer uncovered, stirring occasionally, 10 minutes. Turn into 2-quart casserole.

4. Prepare corn muffin mix according to package directions. Spoon evenly over casserole.

5. Bake uncovered 15 minutes or until corn topping is golden and filling is hot.   *Makes about 6 servings*

1 tablespoon BERTOLLI®
   Olive Oil
1 small onion, chopped
1 pound ground beef
1 envelope LIPTON®
   RECIPE SECRETS®
   Onion Soup Mix*
1 can (14½ ounces) stewed
   tomatoes, undrained
½ cup water
1 can (15 to 19 ounces)
   red kidney beans,
   rinsed and drained
1 package (8½ ounces)
   corn muffin mix

Also terrific with LIPTON® RECIPE SECRETS® Fiesta Herb with Red Pepper, Onion Mushroom, Beefy Onion or Beefy Mushroom Soup Mix.

Meatballs in Burgundy Sauce

60 frozen fully cooked
meatballs
3 cups chopped onions
1½ cups water
1 cup red wine
2 packages (about 1 ounce
each) brown gravy mix
¼ cup ketchup
1 tablespoon dried oregano
1 package (8 ounces) curly
noodles

Slow Cooker Directions

1. Combine meatballs, onions, water, wine, gravy mix, ketchup and oregano in slow cooker; stir to blend.

2. Cover; cook on HIGH 5 hours.

3. Meanwhile cook noodles according to package directions. Serve meatballs with noodles. *Makes 6 to 8 servings*

Beef in a Hurry

Veg•All® Beef & Cheddar Bake

1. Preheat oven to 350°F.

2. In large mixing bowl, combine Veg•All, cheese, macaroni, ground beef, onion and pepper; mix well. Pour mixture into large casserole.

3. Bake for 30 to 35 minutes. Serve hot.

Makes 4 to 6 servings

2 cans (15 ounces each) VEG•ALL® Original Mixed Vegetables, drained
3 cups shredded Cheddar cheese
2 cups cooked elbow macaroni
1 pound extra-lean ground beef, cooked and drained
½ cup chopped onion
¼ teaspoon black pepper

1 can (10 ounces)
    enchilada sauce
2 packages (about
    6 ounces each)
    refrigerated fully
    cooked seasoned beef
    steak strips*
4 (8-inch) flour tortillas
½ cup canned condensed
    nacho cheese soup *or*
    ½ cup chile-flavored
    cheese spread
1½ cups (6 ounces) shredded
    Mexican cheese blend

*Fully cooked beef strips can be found
in the refrigerated prepared meats
section of the supermarket.*

Beef in a Hurry

Southwestern Enchiladas

1. Preheat oven to 350°F. Spread half enchilada sauce in 9-inch glass baking dish; set aside.

2. Divide beef evenly down center of each tortilla. Top with 2 tablespoons cheese soup. Roll up tortillas; place seam-side down in baking dish. Pour remaining enchilada sauce evenly over tortillas. Sprinkle with cheese. Bake 20 to 25 minutes or until heated through.   *Makes 4 servings*

Hearty Shepherd's Pie

1. Preheat oven to 375°F. Cook meat in large oven-proof skillet until browned; drain. Stir in *1 cup* French Fried Onions, soup, *½ cup water,* seasoning and *¼ teaspoon each salt and pepper.*

2. Spoon vegetables over beef mixture. Top with mashed potatoes.

3. Bake 20 minutes or until hot. Sprinkle with remaining *1 cup* onions. Bake 2 minutes or until golden.   *Makes 6 servings*

1½ pounds ground beef

2 cups *French's®* French Fried Onions, divided

1 can (10¾ ounces) condensed tomato soup

2 teaspoons Italian seasoning

1 package (10 ounces) frozen mixed vegetables, thawed

3 cups hot mashed potatoes

Beef in a Hurry

No-Hassle Chicken

Easy Cajun Chicken Stew

2 tablespoons vegetable oil
1 red bell pepper, diced
1 stalk celery, sliced
1 can (about 14 ounces) diced tomatoes with roasted garlic and onions
1½ cups chicken broth
1 package (about 10 ounces) refrigerated fully cooked chicken breast strips
1 cup canned kidney beans, rinsed and drained
1 pouch (about 9 ounces) New Orleans style chicken-flavored ready-to-serve rice mix
¼ teaspoon hot red pepper sauce
¼ cup chopped green onions

1. Heat oil in Dutch oven over medium-high heat. Add bell pepper and celery. Cook and stir 3 minutes. Add tomatoes and chicken broth; bring to a boil.

2. Cut chicken into bite-size pieces. Add chicken, kidney beans, rice mix and pepper sauce. Reduce heat to low. Cover; cook 7 minutes. Stir in onions. Remove from heat. Cover; let stand 2 to 3 minutes to thicken.

Makes 4 servings

Tip: If canned diced tomatoes with garlic and onions aren't available, substitute 1 can (about 14 ounces) diced tomatoes, 1 teaspoon minced garlic and ¼ cup chopped onions to the bell pepper mixture.

Asian Noodles with Vegetables and Chicken

1 tablespoon vegetable oil
2 cups sliced mushrooms
2 cups fresh snow peas
2 packages (1.6 ounces each) garlic and vegetable instant rice noodle soup mix
2 cups boiling water
2 packages (6 ounces each) refrigerated fully cooked chicken breast strips, cut into pieces
¼ teaspoon red pepper flakes
2 tablespoons fresh lime juice
1 tablespoon soy sauce
2 tablespoons chopped cilantro

1. Heat oil in large skillet over medium-high heat. Add mushrooms and snow peas; cook 2 to 3 minutes or until peas are crisp-tender. Remove from skillet; set aside.

2. Break up noodles in soup mix. Add noodles, 1 seasoning packet, water, chicken and pepper flakes to skillet; mix well. Cook over medium-high heat 5 to 7 minutes or until liquid thickens. Stir in reserved vegetables, lime juice and soy sauce. Sprinkle with cilantro.   *Makes 4 servings*

Chicken Casserole Olé

1. Spray large skillet with nonstick cooking spray. Add chicken; cook over medium-high heat 12 to 15 minutes or until lightly browned on both sides and chicken is no longer pink in center.

2. Add water, beans with liquid, salsa and bell pepper. Bring to a boil; add rice and 1 cup cheese. Cover; remove from heat and let stand 5 minutes or until liquid is absorbed. Top with tortilla chips and remaining 1 cup cheese; let stand, covered, 3 to 5 minutes or until cheese is melted.

Makes 6 servings

12 boneless, skinless chicken tenders
2 cups water
1 can (15 ounces) mild chili beans, undrained
1 cup salsa
½ cup chopped green bell pepper
2 cups UNCLE BEN'S® Instant Rice
2 cups (8 ounces) shredded Mexican cheese blend, divided
2 cups bite-size tortilla chips

8 ounces uncooked pasta
1 can (15 ounces) chunky Italian-style tomato sauce
1 cup chopped green bell pepper
1 cup sliced onion
1 cup sliced mushrooms
  Nonstick cooking spray
4 boneless skinless chicken breasts (about 1 pound)
  Salt and black pepper

Chicken Cacciatore

1. Cook pasta according to package directions; drain.

2. While pasta is cooking, combine tomato sauce, bell pepper, onion and mushrooms in microwavable dish. Cover loosely with plastic wrap or waxed paper; microwave on HIGH 6 to 8 minutes, stirring halfway through cooking time.

3. While sauce mixture is cooking, coat large skillet with cooking spray. Heat over medium-high heat. Cook chicken breasts 3 to 4 minutes per side or until lightly browned.

4. Add sauce mixture to skillet; season with salt and pepper. Reduce heat to medium; simmer 12 to 15 minutes. Serve over pasta. *Makes 4 servings*

Green Chili-Chicken Casserole

1. Preheat oven to 325°F. Grease 13×9-inch casserole.

2. Combine chicken, enchilada sauce, soup, sour cream and chiles in large skillet. Cook and stir over medium-high heat until warm.

3. Heat oil in separate deep skillet. Fry tortillas just until soft; drain on paper towels. Place 4 tortillas on bottom of prepared casserole. Layer with ⅓ of chicken mixture and ½ cup cheese. Repeat layers twice.

4. Bake 15 to 20 minutes or until cheese is melted and casserole is heated through.   *Makes 6 servings*

Tip: Shredded Mexican cheese blend can be substituted for Colby-Jack cheese.

4 cups shredded cooked chicken
1½ cups green enchilada sauce
1 can (10¾ ounces) condensed cream of chicken soup, undiluted
1 container (8 ounces) sour cream
1 can (4 ounces) diced mild green chiles
½ cup vegetable oil
12 (6-inch) corn tortillas
1½ cups (6 ounces) shredded Colby-Jack cheese, divided

1 (6.9-ounce) package
   RICE-A-RONI® Chicken
   Flavor
2 tablespoons margarine
   or butter
1 teaspoon dried basil
4 boneless, skinless
   chicken breast halves
   (about 1 pound)
2 cups broccoli flowerets
1 tomato, chopped
1 cup (4 ounces) shredded
   mozzarella or Cheddar
   cheese

Quick & Easy Broccoli Chicken

1. In large skillet over medium heat, sauté rice-vermicelli mix with margarine until vermicelli is golden brown.

2. Slowly stir in 2 cups water, basil and Special Seasonings. Bring to a boil. Place chicken over rice. Reduce heat to low. Cover; simmer 10 minutes.

3. Stir in broccoli and tomato. Cover; simmer 10 minutes or until rice is tender and chicken is no longer pink inside. Sprinkle with cheese. Cover; let stand 3 minutes or until cheese is melted.   *Makes 4 servings*

Tip: If you prefer, use green beans or whole-kernel corn instead of broccoli.

No-Hassle Chicken

Warm Chicken & Couscous Salad

1. Heat oil in large nonstick skillet over medium-high heat. Toss chicken with Cajun seasoning. Add chicken and garlic to skillet; cook and stir 3 minutes or until chicken is cooked through.

2. Add broth and mixed vegetables to skillet; bring to a boil. Stir in couscous. Remove from heat. Cover; let stand 5 minutes. Stir in spinach; transfer to plates. Drizzle with dressing.   *Makes 4 servings*

Serving Suggestion: A side of fresh fruit, such as melon wedges, makes this quick salad into a satisfying meal.

1 tablespoon olive oil
12 ounces chicken tenders
   or boneless skinless
   chicken breasts, cut
   into strips
2 teaspoons Cajun or
   blackened seasoning
1 teaspoon minced garlic
1 can (about 14 ounces)
   chicken broth
2 cups frozen broccoli,
   carrot and red bell
   pepper blend
1 cup uncooked couscous
3 cups packed torn spinach
   leaves
¼ cup poppy seed dressing

Chicken Caesar Tetrazzini

Cook spaghetti according to package directions. Drain and combine with chicken, broth, dressing and mushrooms in a large mixing bowl. Place mixture in a 2-quart casserole. Mix together cheese and bread crumbs; sprinkle over spaghetti mixture. Bake at 350°F. for 25 minutes or until casserole is hot and bubbly. *Makes 4 servings*

8 ounces uncooked spaghetti
2 cups shredded or cubed cooked chicken
1 cup chicken broth
1 cup HIDDEN VALLEY® Caesar Dressing
1 jar (4½ ounces) sliced mushrooms, drained
½ cup grated Parmesan cheese
2 tablespoons dry bread crumbs

No-Hassle Chicken

Quick Hot and Sour Chicken Soup

1. Cut chicken into bite-size pieces. Combine chicken, chicken broth, water, rice mix, jalapeño pepper, onions and soy sauce in large saucepan. Bring to a boil over high heat. Reduce heat to low. Cover; simmer 20 minutes or until rice is tender; stirring occasionally.

2. Stir in lime juice; sprinkle with cilantro.

Makes 4 servings

1 package (about 10 ounces) refrigerated fully cooked chicken breast strips
2 cups chicken broth
2 cups water
1 package (about 10 ounces) chicken-flavored rice and vermicelli mix
1 large jalapeño pepper,* minced
2 green onions, chopped
1 tablespoon soy sauce
1 tablespoon lime juice
1 tablespoon minced cilantro (optional)

*Jalapeño peppers can sting and irritate the skin; wear rubber gloves when handling peppers and do not touch eyes.

No-Hassle Chicken

Chicken and Linguine in Creamy Tomato Sauce

1 tablespoon olive oil
1 pound boneless, skinless chicken breasts, cut into ½-inch strips
1 jar (1 pound 10 ounces) RAGÚ® Old World Style® Pasta Sauce
2 cups water
8 ounces linguine or spaghetti
½ cup whipping or heavy cream
1 tablespoon chopped fresh basil leaves *or* ½ teaspoon dried basil leaves, crushed

1. In 12-inch skillet, heat olive oil over medium heat and brown chicken. Remove chicken and set aside.

2. In same skillet, stir in Ragú Pasta Sauce and water. Bring to a boil over high heat. Stir in uncooked linguine and return to a boil. Reduce heat to low and simmer covered, stirring occasionally, 15 minutes or until linguine is tender.

3. Stir in cream and basil. Return chicken to skillet and cook 5 minutes or until chicken is thoroughly cooked.

Makes 4 servings

No-Hassle Chicken

Artichoke-Olive Chicken Bake

1. Preheat oven to 350°F. Spray 2-quart casserole with nonstick cooking spray.

2. Cook pasta according to package directions until al dente. Drain.

3. Heat oil in large deep skillet over medium heat until hot. Add onion and bell pepper; cook and stir 1 minute. Add pasta, chicken, tomatoes, artichokes, olives and Italian seasoning; mix until blended.

4. Place half of chicken mixture in prepared dish; sprinkle with half of cheese. Top with remaining chicken mixture and cheese.

5. Bake, covered, 35 minutes or until hot and bubbly.   *Makes 8 servings*

1½ cups uncooked rotini
1 tablespoon olive oil
1 medium onion, chopped
½ green bell pepper, chopped
2 cups shredded cooked chicken
1 can (about 14 ounces) diced tomatoes with Italian-style herbs
1 can (14 ounces) artichoke hearts, drained and quartered
1 can (6 ounces) sliced black olives, drained
1 teaspoon dried Italian seasoning
2 cups (8 ounces) shredded mozzarella cheese

No-Hassle Chicken

Mini Chicken Pot Pies

1 container (about 16 ounces) refrigerated reduced-fat buttermilk biscuits

1½ cups milk

1 package (1.8 ounces) white sauce mix

2 cups cut-up cooked chicken

1 cup frozen assorted vegetables, partially thawed

2 cups shredded Cheddar cheese

2 cups *French's®* French Fried Onions

1. Preheat oven to 400°F. Separate biscuits; press into 8 (8-ounce) custard cups, pressing up sides to form crust.

2. Whisk milk and sauce mix in medium saucepan. Bring to boiling over medium-high heat. Reduce heat to medium-low; simmer 1 minute, whisking constantly, until thickened. Stir in chicken and vegetables.

3. Spoon about ⅓ cup chicken mixture into each crust. Place cups on baking sheet. Bake 15 minutes or until golden brown. Top each with cheese and French Fried Onions. Bake 3 minutes or until golden. To serve, remove from cups and transfer to serving plates. *Makes 8 servings*

No-Hassle Chicken

Chicken Enchilada Skillet Casserole

• In large skillet, combine vegetables, chicken, tomatoes and seasoning mix; bring to boil over medium-high heat.

• Cover; cook 4 minutes or until vegetables are cooked and mixture is heated through.

• Sprinkle with cheese; cover and cook 2 minutes more or until cheese is melted.

• Serve with chips.   *Makes 4 servings*

1 bag (16 ounces) BIRDS EYE® frozen Farm Fresh Mixtures Broccoli, Corn & Red Peppers
3 cups shredded cooked chicken
1 can (16 ounces) diced tomatoes, undrained
1 package (1¼ ounces) taco seasoning mix
1 cup shredded Monterey Jack cheese
8 ounces tortilla chips

Broccoli, Chicken and Rice Casserole

1. Heat oven to 425°F. In 13×9-inch baking pan, combine rice and contents of seasoning packet. Add boiling water; mix well. Add chicken; sprinkle with garlic powder. Cover and bake 30 minutes.

2. Add broccoli and cheese; continue to bake, covered, 8 to 10 minutes or until chicken is no longer pink in center. *Makes 4 servings*

1 box UNCLE BEN'S®
    COUNTRY INN®
    **Broccoli Rice Au
    Gratin**
2 cups boiling water
4 boneless, skinless
    chicken breasts
    (about 1 pound)
¼ teaspoon garlic powder
2 cups frozen broccoli
1 cup (4 ounces) reduced-
    fat shredded Cheddar
    cheese

No-Hassle Chicken

Chicken Florentine in Minutes

1. Bring water, milk and butter to a boil in large saucepan over medium-high heat. Stir in pasta mixes, spinach and black pepper. Reduce heat to medium. Cook 8 minutes or until pasta is tender, stirring occasionally.

2. Stir in chicken and red peppers. Cook 2 minutes or until hot. Remove from heat. Stir in sour cream.

Makes 4 servings

3 cups water
1 cup milk
2 tablespoons butter
2 packages (about 4 ounces each) fettuccine Alfredo or stroganoff pasta mix
4 cups fresh baby spinach, coarsely chopped
¼ teaspoon black pepper
1 package (about 10 ounces) refrigerated fully cooked chicken breast strips, cut into pieces
¼ cup diced roasted red peppers
¼ cup sour cream

No-Hassle Chicken

Easy Asian Chicken Skillet

2 packages (3 ounces each)
　　chicken flavor instant
　　ramen noodles
1 package (10 ounces)
　　frozen broccoli florets,
　　thawed
1 package (9 ounces)
　　frozen baby carrots,
　　thawed
1 tablespoon vegetable oil
1 pound boneless skinless
　　chicken breasts, cut
　　into thin strips
1 can (8 ounces) sliced
　　water chestnuts,
　　drained
¼ cup stir-fry sauce

1. Remove seasoning packets from noodles. Save one packet for another use.

2. Bring 4 cups water to a boil in large saucepan. Add noodles, broccoli and carrots. Cook on medium-high 5 minutes, stirring occasionally. Drain.

3. Heat oil in large nonstick skillet over medium-high heat. Add chicken; cook and stir until browned, about 8 minutes.

4. Stir in noodle mixture, water chestnuts, stir-fry sauce and 1 seasoning packet; cook until heated through. *Makes 4 to 6 servings*

No-Hassle Chicken

Chicken & Broccoli with Garlic Sauce

1. In 12-inch nonstick skillet, heat oil over medium-high heat and brown chicken. Remove chicken and set aside.

2. In same skillet, add broccoli and soup mix blended with water and soy sauce. Bring to a boil over high heat.

3. Return chicken to skillet. Reduce heat to low and simmer covered 10 minutes or until chicken is thoroughly cooked. Serve, if desired, over hot cooked rice.

Makes 4 servings

1 tablespoon BERTOLLI®
   Olive Oil
4 boneless, skinless
   chicken breast halves
   (about 1¼ pounds)
1 package (10 ounces)
   frozen broccoli florets,
   thawed
1 envelope LIPTON®
   RECIPE SECRETS®
   Savory Herb with
   Garlic Soup Mix
¾ cup water
1 teaspoon soy sauce

No-Hassle Chicken

Scalloped Chicken & Pasta

¼ cup margarine or butter, divided
1 package (6.2 ounces) PASTA RONI® Shells & White Cheddar
2 cups frozen mixed vegetables
⅔ cup milk
2 cups chopped cooked chicken or ham
¼ cup dry bread crumbs

1. Preheat oven to 450°F.

2. In 3-quart saucepan, combine 2¼ cups water and 2 tablespoons margarine. Bring just to a boil. Stir in pasta and frozen vegetables. Reduce heat to medium.

3. Boil, uncovered, stirring frequently, 12 to 14 minutes or until most of water is absorbed. Add Special Seasonings, milk and chicken. Continue cooking 3 minutes.

4. Meanwhile, melt remaining 2 tablespoons margarine in small saucepan; stir in bread crumbs.

5. Transfer pasta mixture to 8- or 9-inch glass baking dish. Sprinkle with bread crumbs. Bake 10 minutes or until bread crumbs are browned and edges are bubbly.

Makes 4 servings

Chicken Pot Pie with Onion Biscuits

1. Preheat oven to 400°F. Prepare white sauce mix according to package directions with 2¼ cups milk; stir in thyme. Mix vegetables, chicken and prepared white sauce in shallow 2-quart casserole.

2. Combine baking mix, ⅔ *cup* French Fried Onions and remaining ½ cup milk in medium bowl until blended. Drop 6 to 8 spoonfuls of dough over chicken mixture.

3. Bake 25 minutes or until biscuits are golden. Sprinkle biscuits with cheese and remaining onions. Bake 3 minutes or until cheese is melted and onions are golden. *Makes 6 servings*

Tip: You may substitute 2 cups cut-up cooked chicken for the roasted, carved chicken breast.

Variation: For added Cheddar flavor, substitute *French's®* **Cheddar French Fried Onions** for the original flavor.

1 package (1.8 ounces) classic white sauce mix
2¾ cups milk, divided
¼ teaspoon dried thyme leaves
1 package (10 ounces) frozen peas and carrots, thawed
1 package (10 ounces) roasted carved chicken breast, cut into bite-size pieces
1 cup all-purpose baking mix
1⅓ cups *French's®* French Fried Onions, divided
½ cup (2 ounces) shredded Cheddar cheese

15 Minute Chicken and Broccoli Risotto

1 tablespoon oil
1 small onion, chopped
2 pouches (about 9 ounces each) ready-to-serve yellow rice
2 cups frozen chopped broccoli
1 package (about 6 ounces) refrigerated fully cooked chicken breast strips, cut into pieces
½ cup chicken broth or water

1. Heat oil in large skillet over medium-high heat. Add onion; cook 3 minutes or until translucent.

2. Knead rice in bag. Add rice, broccoli, chicken and chicken broth to onions. Cover; cook 6 to 8 minutes or until hot, stirring occasionally.

Makes 4 servings

Serving Suggestion: Top with toasted almond slivers for a crunchy texture and delicious flavor.

No-Hassle Chicken

Italian-Style Chicken and Rice

1. Heat oil in large skillet. Add chicken; cook over medium-high heat 10 to 15 minutes or until lightly browned on both sides.

2. Add broth, rice mix, bell pepper and peas; mix well. Bring to a boil. Cover; reduce heat and simmer 10 minutes or until chicken is no longer pink in center. Remove from heat. Sprinkle with cheese; let stand covered 5 minutes or until liquid is absorbed.

Makes 4 servings

1 tablespoon vegetable oil
4 boneless skinless chicken breasts (about 1 pound)
2 cups chicken broth
1 box (about 6 ounces) chicken-flavored rice mix
½ cup chopped red bell pepper
½ cup frozen peas, thawed
¼ cup Romano cheese

No-Hassle Chicken

Lemon Garlic Chicken & Rice

4 boneless, skinless chicken breast halves (about 1 pound)
½ teaspoon paprika
⅛ teaspoon ground black pepper
2 tablespoons margarine or butter, divided
1 (6.9-ounce) package RICE-A-RONI® Chicken & Garlic Flavor
2 teaspoons lemon juice
1 medium red and/or green bell pepper, chopped

1. Sprinkle chicken with paprika and black pepper; set aside. In large skillet over medium heat, melt 1 tablespoon margarine. Add chicken; cook 2 minutes on each side. Remove from skillet; set aside.

2. In same skillet over medium heat, sauté rice-vermicelli mix with remaining 1 tablespoon margarine until vermicelli is golden brown.

3. Slowly stir in 2 cups water, lemon juice and Special Seasonings; bring to a boil. Place chicken over rice. Reduce heat to low. Cover; simmer 15 minutes.

4. Stir in bell pepper. Cover; cook 5 minutes or until rice is tender and chicken is no longer pink inside. *Makes 4 servings*

Tip: No lemon juice in the house? Try orange juice.

Mexicali Chicken Stew

1. Place half of taco seasoning in small bowl. Cut chicken thighs into 1-inch pieces; coat with taco seasoning.

2. Coat large nonstick skillet with cooking spray. Cook and stir chicken 5 minutes over medium heat. Add tomatoes, corn, beans, and remaining taco seasoning; bring to a boil. Reduce heat to medium-low; simmer 10 minutes. Top with tortilla chips before serving.   *Makes 4 servings*

Serving Suggestion: Serve nachos with the stew. Spread tortilla chips on a plate; dot with salsa and sprinkle with cheese. Heat just until the cheese is melted.

1 package (about 1 ounce) taco seasoning mix, divided
12 ounces boneless skinless chicken thighs
Nonstick cooking spray
2 cans (about 14 ounces each) stewed tomatoes with onions, celery and green peppers
1 package (10 ounces) frozen corn
1 package (9 ounces) frozen green beans
4 cups tortilla chips

Green Chile Chicken Enchiladas

2 cups shredded cooked chicken

1½ cups (6 ounces) shredded Mexican cheese blend or Cheddar cheese, divided

½ cup HIDDEN VALLEY® The Original Ranch® Dressing

¼ cup sour cream

2 tablespoons canned diced green chiles, rinsed and drained

4 (9- to 10-inch) flour tortillas, warmed

Mix together chicken, ¾ cup cheese, dressing, sour cream and green chiles in medium bowl. Divide evenly down center of each tortilla. Roll up tortillas and place, seam side down, in 9-inch baking dish. Top with remaining ¾ cup cheese. Bake at 350°F. for 20 minutes or until cheese is melted and lightly browned.

Makes 4 servings

Note: Purchase rotisserie chicken at your favorite store to add great taste and save preparation time.

No-Hassle Chicken

30 Minute Paella

1. Heat oil in large skillet over medium heat. Add rice mix and pepper flakes. Cook and stir 2 minutes or until vermicelli is golden

2. Add water, chicken, shrimp, peas and red pepper. Bring to a boil. Reduce heat to low. Cover; cook 12 to 15 minutes or until rice is tender, stirring occasionally.

Makes 6 servings

2 tablespoons olive oil
1 package (about 10 ounces) chicken-flavored rice and vermicelli mix
¼ teaspoon red pepper flakes
3½ cups water
1 package (about 10 ounces) refrigerated fully cooked chicken breast strips, cut into pieces
1 package (8 ounces) medium raw shrimp, peeled
1 cup frozen peas
¼ cup diced roasted red pepper

No-Hassle Chicken

1 roasted chicken (about
    2 pounds)
8 flour tortillas
2 cups shredded Cheddar
    cheese
1 cup mild green chili salsa
1 cup mild red salsa

Easy Chicken Chalupas

1. Preheat oven to 350°F. Spray 13×9-inch ovenproof dish with nonstick cooking spray.

2. Remove skin and bones from chicken; discard. Shred chicken meat.

3. Place 2 tortillas in bottom of prepared dish, overlapping slightly. Layer tortillas with 1 cup chicken, ½ cup cheese and ¼ cup of each salsa. Repeat layers, ending with cheese and salsas.

4. Bake casserole 25 minutes or until bubbly and hot.   *Makes 6 servings*

Tip: Serve this easy main dish with some custom toppings—many from a salad bar—such as sour cream, chopped cilantro, sliced black olives, sliced green onions and sliced avocado.

Oriental Chicken & Rice

1. In large skillet over medium heat, sauté rice-vermicelli mix with margarine until vermicelli is golden brown.

2. Slowly stir in 2 cups water, chicken, teriyaki sauce, ginger and Special Seasonings; bring to a boil. Reduce heat to low. Cover; simmer 10 minutes.

3. Stir in vegetables. Cover; simmer 5 to 10 minutes or until rice is tender and chicken is no longer pink inside. Let stand 3 minutes.

Makes 4 servings

Tip: Use pork instead of chicken and substitute ¼ cup orange juice for ¼ cup of the water.

1 (6.9-ounce) package RICE-A-RONI® Chicken Flavor
2 tablespoons margarine or butter
1 pound boneless, skinless chicken breasts, cut into thin strips
¼ cup teriyaki sauce
½ teaspoon ground ginger
1 (16-ounce) package frozen Oriental-style mixed vegetables

2 tablespoons olive oil
1 pound boneless, skinless
  chicken breasts, cut
  into 1-inch cubes
2 cloves garlic, finely
  chopped
2 medium potatoes, cut
  into ½-inch cubes
  (about 4 cups)
1 medium red bell pepper,
  cut into large pieces
1 jar (1 pound 10 ounces)
  RAGÚ® Old World
  Style® Pasta Sauce
1 teaspoon dried basil
  leaves, crushed
  Salt and ground black
  pepper to taste

Simmered Tuscan Chicken

In 12-inch skillet, heat olive oil over medium-high heat and cook chicken with garlic until chicken is thoroughly cooked. Remove chicken and set aside.

In same skillet, add potatoes and bell pepper. Cook over medium heat, stirring occasionally, 5 minutes. Stir in remaining ingredients. Bring to a boil over high heat. Reduce heat to low and simmer covered, stirring occasionally, 35 minutes or until potatoes are tender. Return chicken to skillet and heat through.

Makes 6 servings

Simple Stir-Fry

1. Heat oil in large skillet or wok. Add chicken; cook over medium-high heat 6 to 8 minutes or until lightly browned. Add vegetables, soy sauce and honey. Cover and cook 5 to 8 minutes or until chicken is no longer pink in center and vegetables are crisp-tender.

2. Meanwhile, cook rice according to package directions. Serve stir-fry over rice.

Makes 4 servings

1 tablespoon vegetable oil
12 boneless, skinless chicken breast tenderloins, cut into 1-inch pieces
1 bag (1 pound) frozen stir-fry vegetable mix
2 tablespoons soy sauce
2 tablespoons honey
2 (2-cup) bags UNCLE BEN'S® Boil-in-Bag Rice

No-Hassle Chicken

3½ cups uncooked bowtie
    pasta
1 tablespoon vegetable oil
1 cup sliced mushrooms
1 jar (26 ounces)
    herb-flavored
    spaghetti sauce
1 teaspoon pizza seasoning
    blend
3 boneless skinless chicken
    breasts (about
    ¾ pound), quartered
1 cup (4 ounces) shredded
    mozzarella cheese

Pizza Chicken Bake

1. Preheat oven to 350°F. Spray 2-quart round casserole with nonstick cooking spray.

2. Cook pasta according to package directions until al dente. Drain and place in prepared dish.

3. Meanwhile, heat oil in large skillet over medium-high heat. Add mushrooms; cook and stir 2 minutes. Remove from heat. Stir in spaghetti sauce and pizza seasoning.

4. Pour half of spaghetti sauce mixture into casserole; stir until pasta is well coated. Arrange chicken on top of pasta. Pour remaining spaghetti sauce mixture evenly over chicken.

5. Bake, covered, 50 minutes or until chicken is no longer pink in center. Remove from oven; sprinkle with cheese. Cover and let stand 5 minutes before serving.   *Makes 4 servings*

Tip: Serve this casserole with grated Parmesan cheese and red pepper flakes so that everyone can add their own "pizza" seasonings.

No-Hassle Chicken

Tomato, Basil & Broccoli Chicken

1. Sprinkle chicken with salt and pepper, if desired.

2. In large skillet, melt margarine over medium-high heat. Add chicken; cook 2 minutes on each side or until browned. Remove from skillet; set aside, reserving drippings. Keep warm.

3. In same skillet, sauté rice-vermicelli mix in reserved drippings over medium heat until vermicelli is golden brown. Stir in 2½ cups water, Special Seasonings and basil. Place chicken over rice mixture; bring to a boil over high heat.

4. Cover; reduce heat. Simmer 15 minutes. Top with broccoli and tomato.

5. Cover; continue to simmer 5 minutes or until liquid is absorbed and chicken is no longer pink in center. Sprinkle with cheese. Cover; let stand a few minutes before serving.

Makes 4 servings

4 boneless, skinless
   chicken breast halves
   Salt and black pepper
   (optional)
2 tablespoons margarine
   or butter
1 package (6.9 ounces)
   RICE-A-RONI® Chicken
   Flavor
1 teaspoon dried basil
   leaves
2 cups broccoli florets
1 medium tomato, seeded,
   chopped
1 cup (4 ounces) shredded
   mozzarella cheese

No-Hassle Chicken

Sweet and Spicy Chicken Stir-Fry

1½ cups uncooked long-
    grain white rice
1 can (8 ounces)
    DEL MONTE®
    Pineapple Chunks
    In Its Own Juice
4 boneless, skinless
    chicken breast halves,
    cut into bite-size
    pieces
2 tablespoons vegetable oil
1 large green bell pepper,
    cut into strips
¾ cup sweet and sour sauce
⅛ to ½ teaspoon red
    pepper flakes

1. Cook rice according to package directions.

2. Drain pineapple, reserving ⅓ cup juice.

3. Stir-fry chicken in hot oil in large skillet over medium-high heat until no longer pink in center. Add green pepper and reserved pineapple juice; stir-fry 2 minutes or until tender-crisp.

4. Add sweet and sour sauce, red pepper flakes and pineapple; stir-fry 3 minutes or until heated through.

5. Spoon rice onto serving plate; top with chicken mixture. Garnish, if desired.

Makes 4 servings

No-Hassle Chicken

Orange Ginger Chicken & Rice

1. In large skillet, sauté Rice-A-Roni® mix and margarine over medium heat, stirring frequently until vermicelli is golden brown.

2. Stir in 1½ cups water, orange juice, chicken, garlic, ginger, red pepper flakes and Special Seasonings; bring to a boil over high heat.

3. Cover; reduce heat. Simmer 10 minutes.

4. Stir in carrots.

5. Cover; continue to simmer 5 to 10 minutes or until liquid is absorbed and rice is tender.

Makes 4 servings

1 package (6.9 ounces) **RICE-A-RONI® With ⅓ Less Salt Chicken Flavor**
1 tablespoon margarine or butter
1 cup orange juice
¾ pound skinless boneless chicken breasts, cut into thin strips
2 cloves garlic, minced
¼ teaspoon ground ginger
Dash red pepper flakes (optional)
1½ cups carrots, cut into short thin strips *or* 3 cups broccoli flowerets

Meatless Meals

Hearty Minestrone Soup

2 cans (10¾ ounces each) condensed Italian tomato soup
3 cups water
3 cups cooked vegetables, such as zucchini, peas, corn or beans
2 cups cooked ditalini pasta
1⅓ cups *French's*® French Fried Onions

Combine soup and water in large saucepan. Add vegetables and pasta. Bring to a boil. Reduce heat. Cook until heated through, stirring often.

Place French Fried Onions in microwavable dish. Microwave on HIGH 1 minute or until onions are golden.

Ladle soup into individual bowls. Sprinkle with French Fried Onions.

Makes 6 servings

Southwestern Tortilla Stack

1 (30-ounce) can
    vegetarian refried
    beans
½ cup sour cream
1 can (4 ounces) diced
    mild green chilies,
    drained
½ teaspoon ground cumin
3 (10-inch) flour tortillas
1 cup (4 ounces) shredded
    Cheddar cheese

1. Preheat oven to 425°F. Grease 10-inch round casserole dish.

2. Combine beans, sour cream, chilies and cumin; set aside.

3. Place one tortilla in bottom of prepared casserole. Top with half of the bean mixture and one third of the cheese. Top with second tortilla; repeat layers of beans and cheese.

4. Cover with remaining tortilla; sprinkle with remaining cheese. Cover.

5. Bake 20 minutes or until thoroughly heated. Cut into wedges. Serve with salsa, if desired.

Makes 4 to 6 servings

Four Cheese Mac & Cheese

1. Preheat oven to 350° F. Cook macaroni according to package directions. Drain; set aside and keep warm.

2. Heat milk in large saucepan over medium heat to almost boiling. Reduce heat to low. Gradually add cheeses, stirring constantly. Cook and stir about 5 minutes until all cheese has melted.

3. Place macaroni in 4-quart casserole or individual ovenproof dishes. Pour cheese sauce over pasta and stir until well blended. Sprinkle with bread crumbs. Bake 50 to 60 minutes or until browned and bubbly.

Makes 8 servings

1 package (16 ounces) uncooked macaroni
4 cups milk
4 cups (16 ounces) sharp white Cheddar cheese, shredded
4 cups (16 ounces) American cheese, shredded
2 cups (8 ounces) Muenster cheese, shredded
2 cups (8 ounces) mozzarella cheese, shredded
½ cup bread crumbs

Meatless Meals

Cannellini Parmesan Casserole

2 tablespoons olive oil
1 cup chopped onion
2 teaspoons minced garlic
1 teaspoon dried oregano
¼ teaspoon black pepper
2 cans (about 14 ounces each) diced tomatoes with onion and garlic
1 jar (about 14 ounces) roasted red peppers, drained and cut into ½-inch pieces
2 cans (about 15 ounces each) Great Northern beans, rinsed and drained
1 teaspoon dried basil
¾ cup grated Parmesan cheese

1. Heat oil in Dutch oven over medium heat until hot. Add onion, garlic, oregano and black pepper; cook and stir 5 minutes or until onion is tender.

2. Increase heat to high. Add tomatoes and red peppers; cover and bring to a boil.

3. Reduce heat to medium. Stir in beans; cover and simmer 5 minutes, stirring occasionally. Stir in basil and sprinkle with cheese.

Makes 6 servings

Meatless Meals

Indian Vegetable Curry

• Stir curry powder in large skillet over high heat until fragrant, about 30 seconds.

• Stir in potatoes, vegetables, garbanzo beans and tomatoes; bring to a boil. Reduce heat to medium-high; cover and cook 8 minutes.

• Blend broth with cornstarch; stir into vegetables. Cook until thickened.

Makes about 6 servings

Serving Suggestion: Add cooked chicken for a heartier main dish. Serve with white or brown rice.

2 to 3 teaspoons curry powder
1 can (16 ounces) sliced potatoes, drained
1 bag (16 ounces) BIRDS EYE® frozen Broccoli, Cauliflower and Carrots
1 can (15 ounces) garbanzo beans, drained
1 can (14½ ounces) stewed tomatoes
1 can (13¾ ounces) vegetable or chicken broth
2 tablespoons cornstarch

Cheese & Chili Enchiladas

1 package (8 ounces)
   cream cheese, softened
1 package (8 ounces)
   shredded Cheddar
   cheese, divided
1 can (4 ounces) diced
   mild green chiles
¼ cup sliced green onions
6 (6-inch) flour tortillas
1 cup chunky salsa

1. Preheat oven to 350°F. Lightly spray 11×7-inch baking dish with nonstick cooking spray.

2. Beat cream cheese until smooth. Add 1 cup Cheddar cheese, chiles and onions; beat until blended.

3. Spread ¼ cup cream cheese mixture down center of each tortilla; roll up. Place, seam-side down, in prepared baking dish. Pour salsa over tortillas. Sprinkle with remaining 1 cup Cheddar cheese; cover. Bake 20 to 25 minutes or until heated through.

Makes 6 servings

Vegetarian Asian Noodles with Peanut Sauce

1. Cook noodles according to package directions. Drain; set aside.

2. Heat oil in large skillet over medium-high heat. Add snow peas and carrots; cook 2 minutes. Remove from heat.

3. Add onions, water, peanut butter, chili sauce and soy sauce; mix well. Stir in noodles; toss well to coat. Sprinkle with peanuts. Served warm, not hot.

Makes 4 servings

Tip: To save time, use packaged shredded carrots.

½ package (about 9 ounces) uncooked udon noodles* *or* 4 ounces whole wheat spaghetti
1 tablespoon vegetable oil
2 cups fresh snow peas
1 cup shredded carrots
¼ cup chopped green onions
¼ cup hot water
¼ cup peanut butter
2 to 4 tablespoons hot chili sauce with garlic
1 tablespoon soy sauce
¼ cup dry-roasted peanuts

Udon noodles, wheat flour noodles, are usually available in the Asian section of natural food stores or larger supermarkets.

1 can (14 ounces)
  artichoke hearts,
  drained
5 teaspoons olive oil,
  divided
½ cup minced green onions
5 eggs
½ cup (2 ounces) shredded
  Swiss cheese
2 tablespoons grated
  Parmesan cheese
1 tablespoon minced fresh
  savory *or* 1 teaspoon
  dried savory
1 tablespoon minced fresh
  parsley
1 teaspoon salt
  Black pepper

Artichoke Frittata

1. Chop artichoke hearts; set aside.

2. Heat 3 teaspoons olive oil in 10-inch skillet over medium heat. Add green onions; cook until tender. Remove with slotted spoon; set aside.

3. Beat eggs in medium bowl until light. Stir in artichokes, green onions, cheeses, herbs, salt and pepper.

4. Heat 2 teaspoons olive oil in same skillet over medium heat. Pour egg mixture into skillet. Cook 4 to 5 minutes or until bottom is lightly browned. Place large plate over skillet. Invert frittata onto plate. Return frittata, uncooked side down, to skillet. Cook about 4 minutes more or until center is just set. Cut into 6 wedges to serve. *Makes 6 servings*

Meatless Meals

Layered Mexican Tortilla Cheese Casserole

1. In small bowl, combine tomatoes, ¼ cup cilantro and lime juice; set aside.

2. Coat 8-inch square baking dish with cooking spray. Arrange ¼ of tortillas in bottom of dish; spoon ¼ of tomato mixture over tortillas. Top with ¼ of beans, ¼ of corn and ¼ of cheese. Repeat layering 3 more times with remaining tortillas, tomato mixture, beans, corn and cheese.

3. Bake uncovered at 375°F 25 minutes or until cheese is melted and sauce is bubbly. Sprinkle with remaining ¼ cup cilantro. Let stand 10 minutes before serving.

Makes 4 servings

1 can (14½ ounces) Mexican-style stewed tomatoes, undrained
½ cup chopped fresh cilantro, divided
2 tablespoons lime juice
Nonstick cooking spray
6 (6-inch) corn tortillas, torn into 1½-inch pieces
1 can (15 ounces) black beans, rinsed and drained
1 can (8 ounces) whole kernel corn, drained
2 cups (8 ounces) SARGENTO® Mexican Blend Shredded Cheese

Vegetarian Jambalaya

1 tablespoon vegetable oil
½ cup fresh or frozen diced green or red bell pepper
1 can (about 14 ounces) diced tomatoes with green chilies
1 package (12 ounces) ground taco/burrito flavor soy meat substitute, crumbled
1 pouch (about 9 ounces) New Orleans style ready-to-serve jambalaya rice
2 tablespoons water

1. Heat oil in large skillet over medium-high heat. Add bell pepper; cook 3 minutes.

2. Add tomatoes, soy crumbles and rice; mix well. Stir in water. Cook 5 minutes, uncovered, or until hot.

Makes 4 servings

Meatless Meals

Mexican-Style Rice and Cheese

Slow Cooker Directions

1. Grease inside of slow cooker well. Combine beans, tomatoes, 1 cup cheese, rice, onion, cream cheese and garlic in slow cooker; mix well.

2. Cover; cook on LOW 6 to 8 hours.

3. Sprinkle with remaining 1 cup cheese just before serving.

Makes 6 to 8 servings

1 can (15 ounces) Mexican-style beans
1 can (about 14 ounces) diced tomatoes with green chilies, undrained
2 cups (8 ounces) shredded Monterey Jack or Colby cheese, divided
1½ cups uncooked long-grain rice
1 large onion, finely chopped
½ package (4 ounces) cream cheese
3 cloves garlic, minced

Roasted Vegetables with Fettuccine

2 pounds assorted fresh
vegetables*
1 envelope LIPTON®
RECIPE SECRETS®
Savory Herb with
Garlic Soup Mix**
3 tablespoons BERTOLLI®
Olive Oil
½ cup whipping cream or
half-and-half
¼ cup grated Parmesan
cheese
8 ounces fettuccine or
linguine, cooked and
drained

*Use any combination of the
following, cut into 1-inch chunks:
zucchini, yellow squash, red, green or
yellow bell peppers, carrots, celery,
onion and mushrooms.

**Also terrific with LIPTON® Recipe
Secrets® Golden Onion Soup Mix.

Preheat oven to 450°F. In 13×9-inch baking or roasting pan, combine
vegetables, soup mix and oil until evenly coated.

Bake uncovered, stirring once, 20 minutes or until vegetables are tender. Stir
in light cream and cheese until evenly coated.

Toss with hot fettuccine. Serve, if desired, with additional grated Parmesan
cheese and freshly ground black pepper.   *Makes 2 to 4 servings*

Meatless Meals

Quick Veg•All® Enchiladas

Preheat oven to 350°F. Combine Veg•All and beans in medium bowl. Divide mixture and place in center of each tortilla; roll up. Place rolled tortillas in baking dish. Cover tortillas with enchilada sauce and cheese. Bake for 30 minutes. Top with sour cream, green onions, and ripe olives.

Makes 4 servings

Tip: If tortillas unfold as you are assembling them, turn seam-side down.

1 can (15 ounces) VEG•ALL® Original Mixed Vegetables, drained
1 can (15 ounces) refried beans
8 (6-inch) corn tortillas
1 can (10 ounces) enchilada sauce
1 cup shredded cheddar cheese
1 cup sour cream
½ cup chopped green onions
½ cup chopped ripe olives

Meatless Meals

Three Cheese Baked Ziti

Preheat oven to 350°F. In large bowl, combine ricotta cheese, eggs and Parmesan cheese; set aside.

In another bowl, thoroughly combine pasta and Ragú Chunky Gardenstyle Pasta Sauce.

In 13×9-inch baking dish, spoon ½ of the pasta mixture; evenly top with ricotta cheese mixture, then remaining pasta mixture. Sprinkle with mozzarella cheese. Bake 30 minutes or until heated through. Serve, if desired, with additional heated pasta sauce. *Makes 8 servings*

1 container (15 ounces) part-skim ricotta cheese
2 eggs, beaten
¼ cup grated Parmesan cheese
1 box (16 ounces) ziti pasta, cooked and drained
1 jar (1 pound 10 ounces) RAGÚ® Chunky Gardenstyle Pasta Sauce
1 cup shredded mozzarella cheese (about 4 ounces)

Pesto & Tortellini Soup

1. Cook tortellini according to package directions; drain.

2. While pasta is cooking, bring broth to a boil over high heat in covered Dutch oven. Add cooked tortellini, peppers and peas; return broth to a boil. Reduce heat to medium and simmer 1 minute.

3. Remove soup from heat; stir in spinach and pesto. *Makes 6 servings*

Tip: To remove stems from spinach leaves, fold each leaf in half, then pull stem toward top of leaf. Discard stems.

1 package (9 ounces) fresh cheese tortellini

3 cans (about 14 ounces each) chicken broth

1 jar (7 ounces) roasted red peppers, drained and slivered

¾ cup frozen green peas

3 to 4 cups fresh spinach, washed and stems removed

1 to 2 tablespoons pesto *or* ¼ cup grated Parmesan cheese

Meatless Meals

Minestrone Soup

¾ cup small shell pasta

2 cans (about 14 ounces each) vegetable broth

1 can (28 ounces) crushed tomatoes in tomato purée

1 can (15 ounces) white beans, rinsed and drained

1 package (16 ounces) frozen vegetable medley, such as broccoli, green beans, carrots and red peppers

4 to 6 teaspoons prepared pesto

1. Bring 4 cups water to a boil in large saucepan over high heat. Stir in pasta; cook 8 to 10 minutes or until tender. Drain.

2. While pasta is cooking, combine broth, tomatoes and beans in Dutch oven. Cover and bring to a boil over high heat. Reduce heat to low; simmer 3 to 5 minutes.

3. Add vegetables to broth mixture and return to a boil over high heat. Stir in pasta. Simmer until vegetables and pasta are hot. Ladle soup into bowls; spoon about 1 teaspoon pesto in center of each serving.

Makes 4 to 6 servings

Fiesta Broccoli, Rice and Beans

1. Place broccoli and 2 tablespoons water in microwavable dish. Cover loosely with plastic wrap; cook on HIGH 4 to 5 minutes or until crisp-tender.

2. Cook rice according to package directions, adding chili powder to cooking water.

3. Stir salsa and black beans into hot cooked rice. Top each serving of rice and beans with broccoli and cheese.

Makes 4 servings

2 cups frozen broccoli florets
2 cups uncooked instant rice
½ teaspoon chili powder
1 cup salsa or picante sauce
1 can (about 15 ounces) black beans, rinsed and drained
¼ cup (1 ounce) shredded Cheddar or pepper-Jack cheese

Effortless Turkey

Wild Rice Meatball Primavera

1 pound ground turkey
½ cup seasoned bread
    crumbs
1 egg, beaten
2 tablespoons oil
1 can (10¾ ounces)
    condensed cream
    of mushroom soup,
    undiluted
2 cups water
1 package (16 ounces)
    frozen broccoli
    medley, thawed
1 box UNCLE BEN'S®
    Long Grain & Wild
    Rice Fast Cook Recipe

1. Combine turkey, bread crumbs and egg; mix well. Shape into 1¼- to 1½-inch meatballs (about 20 to 22 meatballs).

2. Heat oil in large skillet over medium-high heat until hot. Cook meatballs 6 to 7 minutes or until brown on all sides. Drain on paper towels.

3. Combine soup and water in skillet; bring to a boil. Add meatballs, vegetables and contents of seasoning packet, reserving rice. Cover; reduce heat and simmer 5 minutes, stirring occasionally.

4. Add reserved rice to skillet; mix well. Cover; cook 5 minutes more or until hot. Remove from heat; stir well. Cover and let stand 5 minutes before serving.

Makes 6 servings

Turkey and Stuffing Bake

1 jar (4½ ounces) sliced
    mushrooms
¼ cup butter or margarine
½ cup diced celery
½ cup chopped onion
1¼ cups **HIDDEN VALLEY®**
    The Original Ranch®
    Dressing, divided
⅔ cup water
3 cups seasoned
    stuffing mix
⅓ cup sweetened dried
    cranberries
3 cups coarsely shredded
    cooked turkey (about
    1 pound)

Drain mushrooms, reserving liquid; set aside. Melt butter over medium-high heat in a large skillet. Add celery and onion; sauté for 4 minutes or until soft. Remove from heat and stir in ½ cup dressing, water and reserved mushroom liquid. Stir in stuffing mix and cranberries until thoroughly moistened. Combine turkey, mushrooms and remaining ¾ cup dressing in a separate bowl; spread evenly in a greased 8-inch baking dish. Top with stuffing mixture. Bake at 350°F for 40 minutes or until bubbly and brown.

Makes 4 to 6 servings

Effortless Turkey

One-Dish Meal

Microwave Directions

Prepare rice according to package directions. Spray 1-quart microwave-safe dish with cooking spray; set aside. Place rice in medium bowl. Add ham, cheese and peas; mix lightly. Spoon into prepared dish; smooth into even layer with spoon. Microwave on HIGH 1 minute; stir. Microwave 30 seconds or until thoroughly heated.   *Makes 4 servings*

Conventional Oven Directions: Assemble casserole as directed. Spoon into ovenproof 1-quart baking dish sprayed with vegetable cooking spray. Bake at 350°F until thoroughly heated, about 15 to 20 minutes.

2 bags SUCCESS® Rice
  Vegetable cooking spray
1 cup cubed cooked
  turkey-ham*
1 cup (4 ounces) shredded
  low-fat Cheddar
  cheese
1 cup peas

*Or, use cooked turkey, ham or turkey franks.

Effortless Turkey

Turkey Enchilada Pie

¾ pound ground turkey
2 teaspoons vegetable oil
1 can (14½ ounces) DEL MONTE® Diced Tomatoes with Zesty Mild Green Chilies
1 package (1¼ ounces) taco seasoning mix
½ cup sliced green onions
1 can (2¼ ounces) sliced ripe olives, drained
6 corn tortillas
1½ cups shredded sharp Cheddar cheese

1. Brown meat in oil in large skillet over medium-high heat. Stir in tomatoes and taco seasoning mix.

2. Reduce heat; cover and cook 10 minutes, stirring occasionally. Stir in green onions and olives.

3. Place 1 tortilla in bottom of 2-quart baking dish; cover with about ½ cup meat sauce. Top with about ¼ cup cheese. Repeat, making a six-layer stack.

4. Pour ½ cup water down edge, into bottom of dish. Cover with foil and bake at 425°F 30 minutes or until heated through. Cut into 4 wedges. Garnish with sour cream, if desired. *Makes 4 servings*

Effortless Turkey

Southwestern Turkey Stew

1. Heat oil in large nonstick skillet over medium-high heat. Add onion and garlic; cook and stir 3 minutes or until onion is translucent.

2. Add broth; bring to a boil. Stir in rice mix, corn, tomatoes, turkey and chipotle pepper. Reduce heat to low. Cover; cook 10 to 12 minutes or until rice is tender. Let stand 3 minutes. Garnish with cilantro.

Makes 4 servings

Substitutions: Use 1 can (about 14 ounces) diced tomatoes with jalapeño peppers in place of chipotle pepper. Or, ¼ teaspoon chipotle chili powder and 1 minced jalapeño pepper can also be substituted for the chipotle pepper.

1 tablespoon vegetable oil
1 small onion, chopped
1 clove garlic, minced
2 cups chicken broth
1 package (about 7 ounces) red beans and rice mix
2 cups frozen corn kernels
1 can (about 14 ounces) diced tomatoes
2 cups diced cooked smoked turkey breast
1 to 2 canned chipotle peppers in adobo sauce,* drained and minced
Cilantro (optional)

*Canned chipotle peppers can be found in the Mexican section of most supermarkets or gourmet food stores.

Zesty Turkey Pot Pie

1 tablespoon vegetable oil
1 small onion, chopped
1 jalapeño pepper,* seeded
  and minced
1 pound ground turkey
1 package (16 ounces)
  frozen mixed
  vegetables
½ teaspoon dried thyme
½ teaspoon black pepper
2 cans (10¾ ounces each)
  condensed golden
  cream of mushroom
  soup, undiluted
1 package (11 ounces)
  refrigerated
  breadsticks

*Jalapeño peppers can sting and
irritate the skin. Wear rubber gloves
when handling peppers and do not
touch eyes. Wash hands after handling.

1. Preheat oven to 350°F.

2. Heat oil in large skillet over medium heat. Add onion and jalapeño pepper; cook and stir 5 minutes or until tender. Add turkey; cook, stirring to break up meat. Drain fat.

3. Stir in vegetables, thyme and pepper. Cook 5 minutes or until vegetables are thawed. Stir in soup. Cook 5 to 10 minutes or until mixture is heated through. Spoon turkey mixture into greased 13×9-inch casserole.

4. Pull and stretch breadsticks to lengthen, pressing ends together if necessary to reach across baking dish. Arrange breadsticks in lattice pattern over turkey mixture, trimming ends. Bake 15 to 20 minutes or until breadsticks are golden brown. *Makes 6 servings*

Tip: The turkey mixture must be hot when it is spooned into the casserole to prevent breadstick bottoms from becoming gummy.

MIXED VEGETABLES

Golden
Cream of
Mushroom
Soup

BREADSTICKS

Effortless Turkey

Turkey Kielbasa with Cabbage, Sweet Potatoes and Apples

1. Combine beer, mustard and caraway seeds in large deep skillet. Bring to a boil over high heat. Add cabbage. Reduce heat to medium-low. Cover and cook 5 to 8 minutes or until cabbage is crisp-tender.

2. Add kielbasa, apple and sweet potatoes. Increase heat to high. Bring mixture to a boil. Reduce heat to medium-low. Cover and cook 3 to 5 minutes or until apple is crisp-tender.   *Makes 6 servings*

Favorite recipe from **National Turkey Federation**

1 bottle (12 ounces) dark
  beer or ale
2 tablespoons Dijon
  mustard
½ teaspoon caraway seeds
6 cups coarsely shredded
  cabbage
1 pound fully cooked
  turkey kielbasa or
  smoked turkey
  sausage, cut into
  2-inch pieces
1 Granny Smith apple, cut
  into ¼-inch wedges
1 can (16 ounces) sweet
  potatoes, cut into
  1½-inch cubes

Turkey and Mushroom Wild Rice Casserole

2 tablespoons butter
1 cup sliced mushrooms
1 small onion, chopped
1 stalk celery, chopped
1 can (10¾ ounces)
    condensed cream of
    mushroom soup,
    undiluted
1 pouch (about 10 ounces)
    ready-to-serve
    wild rice
2 cups diced cooked
    turkey breast
1 cup milk
2 tablespoons minced
    chives
¼ teaspoon black pepper
½ cup coarsely chopped
    pecans

1. Preheat oven to 350°F. Melt butter in large nonstick skillet over medium heat. Add mushrooms, onion and celery; cook 5 minutes or until onion is translucent. Stir in soup, rice, turkey, milk, chives and pepper; mix well.

2. Spoon mixture into 2-quart glass baking dish. Sprinkle with pecans. Bake 15 to 18 minutes or until hot and bubbly.   *Makes 4 servings*

Effortless Turkey

Tomato and Turkey Soup with Pesto

1. Cook pasta according to package directions; drain. Set aside.

2. Meanwhile, combine soup, milk, vegetables and pesto in medium saucepan. Bring to a boil over medium heat; reduce heat to low. Simmer, partially covered, 10 minutes or until vegetables are tender. Add pasta and turkey. Cook 3 minutes or until heated through. Sprinkle with cheese just before serving. *Makes 4 servings*

1 cup uncooked rotini pasta

1 can (10¾ ounces) condensed tomato soup, undiluted

1 cup milk

2 cups (8 ounces) frozen Italian-style vegetables

2 tablespoons prepared pesto

1 cup coarsely chopped cooked turkey

2 tablespoons grated Parmesan cheese

Effortless Turkey

Three-Bean Turkey Chili

1 pound ground turkey
1 small onion, chopped
2 cans (about 14 ounces each) diced tomatoes
1 can (15 ounces) chickpeas (garbanzo beans), rinsed and drained
1 can (15 ounces) kidney beans, rinsed and drained
1 can (15 ounces) black beans, rinsed and drained
1 can (8 ounces) tomato sauce
1 can (4 ounces) diced mild green chiles
1 to 2 tablespoons chili powder

Slow Cooker Directions

1. Cook turkey and onion in medium skillet over medium-high heat, stirring to break up meat. Drain fat. Place turkey mixture into slow cooker.

2. Add remaining ingredients and mix well. Cover; cook on HIGH 6 to 8 hours.

Makes 6 to 8 servings

Effortless Turkey

Broccoli, Turkey and Noodle Skillet

1. Melt butter in large nonstick skillet over medium-high heat. Add bell pepper, broccoli and pepper. Cook 5 minutes or until bell pepper is crisp-tender. Add chicken broth and milk. Bring to a boil. Stir in turkey and pasta mix.

2. Reduce heat to low. Cook 8 to 10 minutes or until noodles are tender. Stir in sour cream. Remove from heat. Let stand, uncovered, 5 minutes or until sauce is thickened.

Makes 4 servings

1 tablespoon butter
1 green bell pepper, chopped
1 cup frozen chopped broccoli, thawed
¼ teaspoon black pepper
1½ cups chicken broth
½ cup milk or half-and-half
2 cups diced cooked turkey breast
1 package (about 4 ounces) chicken and broccoli pasta mix
¼ cup sour cream

Turkey and Biscuits

2 cans (10¾ ounces each) condensed cream of chicken soup, undiluted
¼ cup dry white wine
¼ teaspoon poultry seasoning
2 packages (8 ounces each) frozen cut asparagus, thawed
3 cups cubed cooked turkey or chicken
Paprika (optional)
1 can (11 ounces) refrigerated flaky biscuits

1. Preheat oven to 350°F. Spray 13×9-inch baking dish with nonstick cooking spray.

2. Combine soup, wine and poultry seasoning in medium bowl.

3. Arrange asparagus in single layer in prepared dish. Place turkey evenly over asparagus. Spread soup mixture over turkey. Sprinkle lightly with paprika.

4. Cover tightly with foil and bake 20 minutes. Remove from oven. *Increase oven temperature to 425°F.* Top with biscuits and bake, uncovered, 8 to 10 minutes or until biscuits are golden brown.   *Makes 6 servings*

Effortless Turkey

Turkey & Green Bean Casserole

1. Preheat oven to 350°F. Spray 11×7-inch baking dish with nonstick cooking spray.

2. Spread almonds in single layer on baking sheet. Bake 5 minutes or until golden brown, stirring frequently. Set aside.

3. Arrange stuffing cubes in prepared dish; drizzle with broth. Stir to coat bread cubes with broth.

4. Combine soup, milk and pepper in large bowl. Add green beans and turkey; stir until combined. Spoon over stuffing cubes; top with almonds. Bake, uncovered, 30 to 35 minutes or until heated through.

Makes 4 servings

¼ cup slivered almonds
1 package (7 ounces) herb-seasoned stuffing cubes
¾ cup chicken broth
1 can (10¾ ounces) condensed cream of mushroom soup, undiluted
¼ cup milk or half and half
¼ teaspoon black pepper
1 package (10 ounces) frozen French-style green beans, thawed and drained
2 cups diced cooked turkey breast or chicken

Effortless Turkey

Italian-Glazed Pork Chops

1 tablespoon olive oil
8 bone-in pork chops
1 medium zucchini, thinly
  sliced
1 medium red bell pepper,
  chopped
1 medium onion, thinly
  sliced
3 cloves garlic, finely
  chopped
¼ cup dry red wine or beef
  broth
1 jar (1 pound 10 ounces)
  RAGÚ® Chunky Pasta
  Sauce

1. In 12-inch skillet, heat olive oil over medium-high heat and brown chops. Remove chops and set aside.

2. In same skillet, cook zucchini, red bell pepper, onion and garlic, stirring occasionally, 4 minutes. Stir in wine and Ragú Pasta Sauce.

3. Return chops to skillet, turning to coat with sauce. Simmer covered 15 minutes or until chops are tender and barely pink in the center. Serve, if desired, over hot cooked couscous or rice. *Makes 8 servings*

Teriyaki Rib Dinner

1 package (about
  15 ounces) refrigerated
  fully cooked pork back
  ribs in barbecue sauce
2 tablespoons vegetable oil
1 large onion, thinly sliced
4 cups frozen Japanese-
  style stir-fry vegetables
1 can (8 ounces) pineapple
  chunks with juice
¼ cup hoisin sauce
2 tablespoons cider vinegar

1. Remove ribs from package; reserve extra barbecue sauce. Cut into individual ribs; set aside.

2. Heat oil in Dutch oven over medium-high heat. Add onion; cook 3 minutes or until translucent. Add vegetables; cook and stir 4 minutes.

3. Add ribs, reserved sauce, pineapple with juice, hoisin sauce and vinegar to vegetable mixture; mix well. Cover; cook 5 minutes or until hot.

Makes 4 servings

Tip: Substitute fresh diced pineapple from the supermarket produce section.

Rush-Hour Pork

Ham and Cheese Bread Pudding

1. Grease 11×7-inch baking dish. Spread 1 side of each bread slice with butter. Cut into 1-inch cubes; place on bottom of prepared dish. Top with ham; sprinkle with cheese.

2. Beat eggs in medium bowl. Whisk in milk, mustard, salt and pepper. Pour egg mixture evenly over bread mixture. Cover; refrigerate at least 6 hours or overnight.

3. Preheat oven to 350°F. Bake bread pudding, uncovered, 45 to 50 minutes or until puffed and golden brown and knife inserted into center comes out clean. Garnish as desired. Cut into squares. Serve immediately.

Makes 8 servings

1 small loaf (8 ounces) sourdough, country French or Italian bread, cut into 1-inch-thick slices
3 tablespoons butter, softened
8 ounces ham or smoked ham, cubed
2 cups (8 ounces) shredded mild or sharp Cheddar cheese
3 eggs
2 cups milk
1 teaspoon dry mustard
½ teaspoon salt
⅛ teaspoon white pepper

Rush-Hour Pork

Hearty Pork, Apple and Noodle Skillet

2 apples, peeled, cored
2 tablespoons butter, divided
1 small onion, finely chopped
½ package (about 27 ounces) refrigerated garlic and herb marinated pork loin fillet
1½ cups chicken broth
½ cup milk
1 package (about 4 ounces) stroganoff pasta mix
¼ teaspoon black pepper
¼ cup sour cream

1. Cut apples into ¼-inch-thick slices. Melt 1 tablespoon butter in large nonstick skillet over medium heat. Add apples and onion. Cook 5 to 10 minutes or until apples are lightly browned. Remove to small bowl; set aside.

2. Cut ½ pork loin into ½-inch-thick slices. (Reserve remaining pork for another meal.) Melt remaining 1 tablespoon butter in skillet over medium heat. Brown pork in 2 batches, 1 to 2 minutes per side. Do not overcook. Remove to warm platter; repeat with remaining pork.

3. Place broth and milk in skillet; bring to a boil. Add pasta mix, apple mixture and pepper; mix well. Cook over medium heat 10 minutes or until noodles are tender and sauce is slightly thickened. Stir in sour cream. Serve with pork.

Make 4 servings

Rush-Hour Pork

Hawaiian-Roni

1. In small bowl, combine pork and teriyaki sauce; set aside.

2. In large skillet over medium heat, sauté rice-vermicelli mix and onion with margarine until vermicelli is golden brown.

3. Slowly stir in 1 cup water, reserved ¼ cup pineapple juice, carrots, pork mixture and Special Seasonings; bring to a boil. Reduce heat to medium-low. Cover; simmer 15 to 20 minutes or until rice is tender and pork is no longer pink inside.

4. Stir in pineapple chunks. Cover; let stand 5 minutes before serving. Sprinkle with almonds.

Makes 4 servings

Tip: For variety, try sliced chicken or steak instead of pork.

1 pound boneless pork loin chops, cut into 1-inch pieces
¼ cup teriyaki sauce
1 (6.2-ounce) package RICE-A-RONI® Fried Rice
¼ cup chopped onion
2 tablespoons margarine or butter
1 (8-ounce) can pineapple chunks in juice, drained, reserving ¼ cup juice
1 cup sliced carrots
¼ cup slivered almonds, toasted

Rush-Hour Pork

Italian-Style Sausage with Rice

1 pound mild Italian sausage links, cut into 1-inch pieces

1 can (15 ounces) pinto beans, rinsed and drained

1 cup pasta sauce

1 green bell pepper, cut into strips

1 small onion, halved and sliced

½ teaspoon salt

¼ teaspoon black pepper

Hot cooked rice

Chopped fresh basil (optional)

Slow Cooker Directions

1. Brown sausage in large nonstick skillet over medium heat. Drain and discard fat.

2. Place sausage, beans, pasta sauce, bell pepper, onion, salt and black pepper into slow cooker. Cover; cook on LOW 4 to 6 hours.

3. Serve with rice. Garnish with basil.

Makes 4 to 5 servings

PINTO BEANS

Rush-Hour Pork

Ravioli Soup

1. Cook pasta according to package directions; drain.

2. Meanwhile, cook sausage in 5-quart pot over medium-high heat until no longer pink; drain. Add undrained tomatoes, broth and 1¾ cups water; bring to a boil.

3. Reduce heat to low; stir in pasta, beans and green onions. Simmer until heated through. Season with pepper and sprinkle with grated Parmesan cheese, if desired.   *Makes 4 servings*

1 package (9 ounces) fresh
   or frozen cheese
   ravioli or tortellini
¾ pound hot Italian
   sausage, crumbled
1 can (14½ ounces)
   DEL MONTE® Stewed
   Tomatoes - Seasoned
   with Basil, Garlic
   & Oregano
1 can (14½ ounces) beef
   broth
1 can (14½ ounces)
   DEL MONTE® Italian
   Beans, drained
2 green onions, sliced

Rush-Hour Pork

Southern Pork Barbecue Dinner

1 tablespoon vegetable oil
½ cup chopped onion
½ cup chopped celery
½ cup chopped green bell pepper
1 container (about 18 ounces) refrigerated fully cooked shredded pork
1 can (15 ounces) pinto beans or black-eyed peas, rinsed and drained
1 can (8 ounces) tomato sauce
2 tablespoons Dijon mustard

1. Heat oil in large skillet over medium-high heat. Add onion, celery and bell pepper; cook and stir 5 minutes or until tender.

2. Stir in pork, beans, tomato sauce and mustard. Cook over low heat 5 to 10 minutes or until hot.   *Makes 4 to 6 servings*

Variation: To make a sandwich, omit the beans and serve on buns.

Rush-Hour Pork

New Orleans Rice and Sausage

Heat sausage in large skillet 2 to 3 minutes.

Add tomatoes, water, rice and TABASCO® Pepper Sauce; mix well.

Add vegetables; mix well. Cover and cook over medium heat 5 to 7 minutes or until rice is tender and vegetables are heated through.

Makes 6 servings

½ pound smoked sausage,*
   cut into slices
1 can (14½ ounces) stewed
   tomatoes, Cajun- or
   Italian-style
¾ cup water
1¾ cups uncooked instant
   rice
   Dash TABASCO®**
   Pepper Sauce or
   to taste
1 bag (16 ounces)
   BIRDS EYE® frozen
   Broccoli, Corn and
   Red Peppers

*For a spicy dish, use andouille sausage. Any type of kielbasa or turkey kielbasa can also be used.

**Tabasco® is a registered trademark of McIlhenny Company.

Mexicali Cornbread Casserole

2½ cups frozen mixed vegetables, thawed

1½ cups cubed **HILLSHIRE FARM®** Ham

1 package (10 ounces) cornbread stuffing mix

2 cups milk

3 eggs, lightly beaten

Salt and black pepper to taste

½ cup (2 ounces) shredded taco-flavored cheese

Preheat oven to 375°F.

Combine mixed vegetables, Ham and stuffing mix in small casserole; set aside. Combine milk, eggs, salt and pepper in medium bowl; pour over ham mixture. Bake, covered, 45 minutes. Top with cheese; bake, uncovered, 3 minutes or until cheese is melted.

Makes 4 servings

Skillet Sausage and Bean Stew

1. Combine sausage and onion in large nonstick skillet; cook and stir over medium-high heat 5 to 7 minutes or until meat is cooked through. Drain fat.

2. Stir in potatoes, beans, water, bouillon, oregano and red pepper; reduce heat to medium. Cover; simmer 15 minutes, stirring occasionally.

Makes 4 servings

1 pound spicy Italian sausage, cut into $\frac{1}{2}$-inch pieces

$\frac{1}{2}$ onion, chopped

2 cups frozen O'Brien potatoes with onions and peppers

1 can (15 ounces) pinto beans, undrained

$\frac{3}{4}$ cup water

1 teaspoon beef bouillon granules *or* 1 beef bouillon cube

1 teaspoon dried oregano

$\frac{1}{8}$ teaspoon ground red pepper

Rush-Hour Pork

Stuffed Green Peppers

6 medium to large green
bell peppers
1 pound BOB EVANS®
Original Recipe Roll
Sausage
2 cups tomato sauce
2 cups water
1 small onion, chopped
1 cup uncooked rice
Sliced green onion
(optional)

Preheat oven to 350°F. Slice off tops from peppers; scrape out centers to remove seeds and membranes. Combine all remaining ingredients except green onion in medium bowl; mix well. Evenly stuff peppers with sausage mixture. Place in lightly greased deep 3-quart casserole dish. Bake, covered, 20 minutes. Uncover; bake 5 to 10 minutes more or until peppers are fork-tender and filling is set. Garnish with green onion, if desired. Serve hot. Refrigerate leftovers. *Makes 6 servings*

Tip: For a pretty presentation, slice 6 small peppers lengthwise in half through stem; scrape out centers to remove seeds and membranes. Proceed as directed, serving 2 halves to each guest.

Serving Suggestion: Serve with mixed salad of carrot, radish and cucumber slices drizzled with a vinaigrette.

Italian Sausage and Rice Frittata

1. Whisk together eggs, milk and salt in medium bowl. Set aside.

2. Preheat oven to 325°F. Cook sausage about 7 minutes in 11-inch ovenproof nonstick skillet over high heat until no longer pink.

3. Reduce heat to medium-low. Stir in rice, stewed tomatoes with their juices, breaking up any large pieces, and Italian seasoning. Sprinkle evenly with 1 cup cheese.

4. Pour egg mixture into skillet; stir gently to distribute egg. Cover and cook 15 minutes or until eggs are just set.

5. Remove from heat. Sprinkle remaining ½ cup cheese over frittata. Bake about 10 minutes more or until puffed and cheese is melted.

6. Remove skillet from oven. Cover and let stand 5 minutes. Cut into 6 wedges before serving.

Makes 6 servings

Tip: Choose a blend of shredded mozzarella and provolone for this frittata, or the blend of your choice.

7 large eggs
¾ cup milk
½ teaspoon salt
½ pound mild or hot Italian sausage, casing removed and sausage broken into small pieces
1½ cups uncooked UNCLE BEN'S® Instant Brown Rice
1 can (14½ ounces) Italian-style stewed tomatoes
¼ teaspoon Italian herb seasoning
1½ cups (6 ounces) shredded Italian cheese blend, divided

Harvest Ham Supper

6 carrots, sliced in half lengthwise

3 sweet potatoes, sliced in half lengthwise

1 pound boneless ham (about 1½ pounds)

1 cup maple syrup

Slow Cooker Directions

1. Place carrots and potatoes in bottom of slow cooker to form rack. Place ham on top of vegetables. Pour syrup over ham and vegetables.

2. Cover; cook on LOW 6 to 8 hours.

Makes 6 servings

Rush-Hour Pork

Polish Reuben Casserole

1. Preheat oven to 350°F. Grease 13×9-inch baking dish.

2. Combine soup, milk, onion and mustard in medium bowl; blend well. Spread sauerkraut in prepared dish. Top with uncooked noodles. Spoon soup mixture evenly over noodles; cover with sausage. Top with cheese. Combine bread crumbs and butter in small bowl; sprinkle over casserole.

3. Cover dish tightly with foil. Bake about 1 hour or until noodles are tender. Garnish as desired. *Makes 8 to 10 servings*

2 cans (10¾ ounces each) condensed cream of mushroom soup
1⅓ cups milk
½ cup chopped onion
1 tablespoon prepared mustard
2 cans (16 ounces each) sauerkraut, rinsed and drained
1 package (8 ounces) uncooked medium noodles
1½ pounds Polish sausage, cut into ½-inch pieces
2 cups (8 ounces) shredded Swiss cheese
¾ cup whole wheat bread crumbs
2 tablespoons butter, melted

Rush-Hour Pork

Sweet and Savory Sausage Casserole

2 sweet potatoes, peeled and cut into 1-inch cubes

2 apples, peeled, cored and cut into 1-inch cubes

1 medium onion, cut into thin strips

2 tablespoons vegetable oil

2 teaspoons Italian seasoning

1 teaspoon garlic powder

½ teaspoon salt

½ teaspoon black pepper

1 pound cooked Italian sausage, cut into ½-inch pieces

1. Preheat oven to 400°F. Spray 13×9-inch baking pan with nonstick cooking spray.

2. Combine potatoes, apples, onion, oil, Italian seasoning, garlic powder, salt and pepper in large bowl. Toss to coat evenly. Place potato mixture into prepared pan. Bake, covered, 30 minutes. Add sausage to potato mixture; bake 5 to 10 minutes or until sausage is heated through and potatoes are tender.

Makes 4 to 6 servings

Rush-Hour Pork

Brunswick Stew

1. Spray large saucepan with cooking spray; heat over medium heat until hot. Add ham and onion; cook 5 minutes or until ham is browned. Stir in flour; cook over medium to medium-low heat 1 minute, stirring constantly.

2. Stir in tomatoes, mixed vegetables and broth; bring to a boil. Reduce heat to low; simmer, covered, 5 to 8 minutes or until vegetables are tender. Simmer, uncovered, 5 to 8 minutes or until slightly thickened. Season to taste with salt and pepper. *Makes 4 servings*

Serving Suggestion: Brunswick Stew is excellent served over rice or squares of cornbread.

Nonstick cooking spray
12 ounces smoked ham or cooked chicken breast, cut into ¾- to 1-inch cubes
1 cup sliced onion
4½ teaspoons all-purpose flour
1 can (about 14 ounces) stewed tomatoes
2 cups frozen mixed vegetables for soup (such as okra, lima beans, potatoes, celery, corn, carrots, green beans and onions)
1 cup chicken broth
Salt
Black pepper

Rush-Hour Pork

Italian Sausage Supper

1 pound mild Italian
 sausage, casing
 removed
1 cup chopped onion
3 medium zucchini, sliced
 (about 1½ cups)
1 can (6 ounces)
 CONTADINA®
 Tomato Paste
1 cup water
1 teaspoon dried basil
 leaves, crushed
½ teaspoon salt
3 cups cooked rice
1 cup (4 ounces) shredded
 mozzarella cheese
¼ cup (1 ounce) grated
 Romano cheese

1. Brown sausage with onion in large skillet, stirring to break up sausage; drain, reserving 1 tablespoon drippings.

2. Spoon sausage mixture into greased 2-quart casserole dish. Add zucchini to skillet; sauté for 5 minutes or until crisp-tender.

3. Combine tomato paste, water, basil and salt in medium bowl. Stir in rice. Spoon over sausage mixture. Arrange zucchini slices on top; sprinkle with mozzarella and Romano cheeses.

4. Cover. Bake in preheated 350°F oven for 20 minutes.

Makes 6 servings

Rush-Hour Pork

Ham and Potato au Gratin

Preheat oven to 350°F.

Melt butter in large saucepan over medium heat; stir in flour. Add milk. Cook and stir until bubbly; cook 1 minute more. Remove from heat. Stir in cheese and mustard; set aside.

Place ½ of Ham in ungreased medium casserole. Top with ½ of potatoes and ½ of milk mixture. Spoon spinach over top. Repeat layers with remaining ham, potatoes and milk mixture.

Bake, uncovered, 30 minutes or until heated through.   *Makes 8 servings*

3 tablespoons butter or margarine
3 tablespoons all-purpose flour
2 cups milk
1½ cups (6 ounces) shredded Cheddar cheese
1 tablespoon Dijon mustard
2 cups HILLSHIRE FARM® Ham, cut into thin strips
1 package (24 ounces) frozen shredded hash brown potatoes, thawed
1 package (10 ounces) frozen chopped spinach, thawed and drained

Sausage and Broccoli Noodle Casserole

1 jar (1 pound) RAGÚ®
   Cheesy! Classic
   Alfredo Sauce
⅓ cup milk
1 pound sweet Italian
   sausage, cooked and
   crumbled
1 package (9 ounces)
   frozen chopped
   broccoli, thawed
8 ounces egg noodles,
   cooked and drained
1 cup shredded Cheddar
   cheese (about
   4 ounces), divided
¼ cup chopped roasted red
   peppers

1. Preheat oven to 350°F. In large bowl, combine Alfredo Sauce and milk. Stir in sausage, broccoli, noodles, ¾ cup cheese and roasted peppers.

2. In 13×9-inch baking dish, evenly spread sausage mixture. Sprinkle with remaining ¼ cup cheese.

3. Bake 30 minutes or until heated through.   *Makes 6 servings*

Tip: Substitute sausage with equal amounts of vegetables for a hearty vegetarian entrée.

Rush-Hour Pork

Pork with Savory Apple Stuffing

1. Preheat oven to 375°F. Combine stuffing mix, broth, apple, celery and ²⁄₃ cup French Fried Onions in large bowl. Spoon into bottom of greased shallow 2-quart baking dish. Arrange chops on top of stuffing.

2. Combine sweet & sour sauce with mustard in small bowl. Pour over pork. Bake 40 minutes or until pork is no longer pink in center.

3. Sprinkle with remaining onions. Bake 5 minutes or until onions are golden.

Makes 4 servings

1 package (6 ounces) corn bread stuffing mix
1 can (14½ ounces) chicken broth
1 small apple, peeled, cored and chopped
¼ cup chopped celery
1⅓ cups *French's®* French Fried Onions, divided
4 boneless pork chops, ¾ inch thick (about 1 pound)
½ cup peach-apricot sweet & sour sauce
1 tablespoon *French's®* Honey Dijon Mustard

Lit'l Smokies 'n' Macaroni 'n' Cheese

Preheat oven to 350°F.

Combine prepared macaroni and cheese, Lit'l Smokies, soup, milk and parsley, if desired, in medium bowl. Pour into small greased casserole. Sprinkle Cheddar cheese over top. Bake, uncovered, 20 minutes or until heated through.

Makes 8 servings

1 package (7¼ ounces) macaroni and cheese mix, prepared according to package directions
1 pound HILLSHIRE FARM® Lit'l Smokies
1 can (10¾ ounces) condensed cream of celery or mushroom soup, undiluted
⅓ cup milk
1 tablespoon minced parsley (optional)
1 cup (4 ounces) shredded Cheddar cheese

Rush-Hour Pork

Carolina Baked Beans & Pork Chops

1. Preheat oven to 400°F. Combine all ingredients *except pork chops* in 3-quart shallow baking dish; mix well. Arrange chops on top, turning once to coat with sauce.

2. Bake, uncovered, 30 to 35 minutes or until pork is no longer pink in center. Stir beans around chops once during baking. Serve with green beans or mashed potatoes, if desired.   *Makes 6 servings*

2 cans (16 ounces each) pork and beans
½ cup chopped onion
½ cup chopped green bell pepper
¼ cup *French's® Classic Yellow®* Mustard
¼ cup packed light brown sugar
2 tablespoons *French's®* Worcestershire Sauce
1 tablespoon *Frank's® RedHot®* Original Cayenne Pepper Sauce
6 boneless pork chops (1 inch thick)

Tuscan Pot Pie

1. Preheat oven to 425°F. Remove sausage from casings. Brown sausage in medium ovenproof skillet, stirring to break up meat. Drain fat.

2. Add spaghetti sauce, beans and thyme to skillet. Simmer, uncovered, over medium heat 5 minutes. Remove from heat; stir in cheese.

3. Unroll crescent dough; divide into triangles. Arrange in spiral with points of dough toward center, covering sausage mixture completely. Bake 12 minutes or until crust is golden brown and meat mixture is bubbly.

Makes 4 to 6 servings

Tip: To remove a sausage casing, use a pairing knife to slit the casing at one end. Be careful not to cut through the sausage. Grasp the cut edge and gently pull the casing away from the sausage.

- ¾ pound sweet or hot Italian sausage
- 1 jar (26 to 28 ounces) chunky vegetable or mushroom spaghetti sauce
- 1 can (19 ounces) cannellini beans, rinsed and drained
- ½ teaspoon dried thyme
- 1½ cups (6 ounces) shredded mozzarella cheese
- 1 package (8 ounces) refrigerated crescent dinner rolls

Bacon & Potato Frittata

1. Preheat broiler. Place potatoes in medium microwavable bowl; microwave on HIGH 1 minute.

2. Melt butter in large ovenproof skillet over medium-high heat. Swirl butter up side of pan to prevent eggs from sticking. Add potatoes; cook 3 minutes, stirring occasionally.

3. Beat eggs in medium bowl. Add bacon, half-and-half, salt and pepper; mix well. Pour egg mixture into skillet; reduce heat to medium. Stir gently to incorporate potatoes. Cover and cook 6 minutes or until eggs are set at edges (top will still be wet).

4. Transfer skillet to broiler. Broil 4 inches from heat about 1 to 2 minutes or until center is set and frittata is golden brown. Cut into wedges.

Makes 4 servings

Serving Suggestion: Garnish frittata with red bell pepper strips, chopped chives and salsa.

2 cups frozen O'Brien-style potatoes with onions and peppers
3 tablespoons butter or margarine
5 eggs
½ cup canned real bacon pieces
¼ cup half-and-half or milk
⅛ teaspoon salt
⅛ teaspoon black pepper

Rush-Hour Pork

Hearty Noodle Casserole

1 pound Italian sausage, casings removed
1 jar (26½ ounces) pasta sauce
1 pint (16 ounces) ricotta or cottage cheese
1 package (12 ounces) extra wide egg noodles, cooked
1 package (8 ounces) shredded mozzarella cheese, divided
1 can (4 ounces) sliced mushrooms
½ cup chopped green bell pepper

1. Preheat oven to 350°F. Brown sausage in large skillet over medium-high heat, stirring to break up meat. Drain fat.

2. Combine sauce, sausage, ricotta cheese, noodles, half the mozzarella cheese, mushrooms and bell pepper in large bowl. Spoon into 3-quart or 13×9-inch baking pan. Top with remaining mozzarella cheese.

3. Bake, uncovered, about 25 minutes or until heated through.

Makes 4 to 6 servings

Rush-Hour Pork

Fiesta Rice and Sausage

Slow Cooker Directions

1. Heat oil in large nonstick skillet over medium-high heat. Brown sausage, stirring to break up meat. Add garlic and cumin; cook 30 seconds. Add onions, bell peppers and jalapeño peppers. Cook and stir until onions are tender, about 10 minutes. Place mixture in slow cooker.

2. Stir in beef broth and rice.

3. Cover; cook on LOW 4 to 6 hours or on HIGH 1 to 2 hours.

Makes 10 to 12 servings

1 teaspoon vegetable oil
2 pounds spicy Italian sausage, casings removed
2 cloves garlic, minced
2 teaspoons ground cumin
4 onions, chopped
4 green bell peppers, chopped
3 jalapeño peppers,* seeded and minced
4 cups beef broth
2 packages (6¼ ounces each) long grain and wild rice mix

Jalapeño peppers can sting and irritate the skin; wear rubber gloves when handling peppers and do not touch eyes. Wash hands after handling.

Rush-Hour Pork

8 ounces uncooked rotini pasta

1 bag (16 ounces) frozen vegetable blend (broccoli, cauliflower, red peppers and corn)

4 ounces turkey ham, chopped

1½ cups milk

2 tablespoons all-purpose flour

1¼ cups (5 ounces) shredded Monterey Jack cheese

Black pepper

Creamy Ham and Garden Rotini

1. Preheat oven to 325°F. Spray 11×8-inch baking pan with nonstick cooking spray; set aside. Cook pasta according to package directions; drain. Place in bottom of prepared pan; set aside.

2. Meanwhile, add ½ cup water to large nonstick skillet. Bring to a boil over high heat. Add vegetables; return to a boil. Reduce heat to low; simmer, covered, 4 minutes. Drain. Toss vegetables and ham with pasta; set aside.

3. Combine milk and flour in small bowl; whisk until smooth. Pour milk mixture into same skillet; cook over medium-high heat, stirring constantly, until slightly thickened. Remove from heat. Pour over pasta mixture. Top with cheese; sprinkle with pepper. Cover loosely with foil. Bake 25 to 30 minutes or until heated through.

Makes 4 servings

Rush-Hour Pork

Country Sausage Macaroni and Cheese

Preheat oven to 350°F. Crumble and cook sausage in medium skillet until browned. Drain on paper towels. Combine milk, processed cheese and mustard in medium saucepan; cook and stir over low heat until cheese melts and mixture is smooth. Stir in sausage, tomatoes, mushrooms, green onions and cayenne pepper. Remove from heat.

Cook macaroni according to package directions; drain. Combine hot macaroni and cheese mixture in large bowl; toss until well coated. Spoon into greased shallow 2-quart casserole dish. Cover and bake 15 to 20 minutes. Stir; sprinkle with Parmesan cheese. Bake, uncovered, 5 minutes more. Let stand 10 minutes before serving. Refrigerate leftovers.

Makes 6 to 8 servings

1 pound BOB EVANS® Special Seasonings Roll Sausage

1½ cups milk

12 ounces pasteurized processed Cheddar cheese, cut into cubes

½ cup Dijon mustard

1 cup diced fresh or drained canned tomatoes

1 cup sliced mushrooms

⅓ cup sliced green onions

⅛ teaspoon cayenne pepper

12 ounces uncooked elbow macaroni

2 tablespoons grated Parmesan cheese

No-Fuss Fish

Tuna Tomato Casserole

2 cans (6 ounces each)
   tuna, drained
1 cup mayonnaise
1 small onion, finely
   chopped
¼ teaspoon salt
¼ teaspoon black pepper
1 package (12 ounces)
   uncooked wide egg
   noodles
8 to 10 plum tomatoes,
   sliced ¼ inch thick
1 cup (4 ounces) shredded
   Cheddar or mozzarella
   cheese

1. Preheat oven to 375°F.

2. Combine tuna, mayonnaise, onion, salt and pepper in medium bowl.
Mix well; set aside.

3. Prepare noodles according to package directions, cooking just until tender.
Drain noodles; return to pan.

4. Add tuna mixture to noodles; stir until well combined.

5. Layer half of noodle mixture, half of tomatoes and half of cheese in
13×9-inch baking dish. Press down slightly. Repeat layers with remaining
ingredients.

6. Bake 20 minutes or until cheese is melted and casserole is heated through.

Makes 6 servings

By-the-Sea Casserole

1 bag (16 ounces)
    BIRDS EYE® frozen
    Mixed Vegetables
2 cans (6 ounces each)
    tuna in water, drained
1 cup uncooked instant
    rice
1 can (10¾ ounces) cream
    of celery soup
1 cup 1% milk
1 cup cheese-flavored
    fish-shaped crackers

Microwave Directions

• In medium bowl, combine vegetables and tuna.

• Stir in rice, soup and milk.

• Place tuna mixture in 1½-quart microwave-safe casserole dish; cover and microwave on HIGH 6 minutes. Stir; microwave, covered, 6 to 8 minutes more or until rice is tender.

• Stir casserole and sprinkle with crackers.

Makes 6 servings

Smoked Salmon Hash Browns

1. Combine potatoes, salmon, onion, bell pepper and pepper in bowl; toss gently to mix well.

2. Heat oil in large nonstick skillet over medium-high heat. Add potato mixture; spread to cover surface of skillet. Carefully pat down to avoid oil spatter.

3. Cook 5 minutes or until crisp and browned. Turn over in large pieces. Brown 2 to 3 minutes.   *Makes 4 servings*

3 cups frozen hash brown
   potatoes, thawed
2 pouches (3 ounces each)
   smoked Pacific
   salmon*
½ cup chopped onion
½ cup chopped bell pepper
¼ teaspoon black pepper
2 tablespoons vegetable oil

*Smoked salmon in foil packages can be found in the canned fish section of the supermarket. Do not substitute lox or other fresh smoked salmon.

No-Fuss Fish

Curried Shrimp and Noodles

2 packages (about 1.6 ounces each) curry-flavored instant rice noodle soup mix
1 package (8 ounces) frozen cooked baby shrimp
1 cup frozen bell pepper strips, cut into 1-inch pieces *or* 1 cup frozen peas
¼ cup chopped green onions
¼ teaspoon salt
¼ teaspoon black pepper
1 to 2 tablespoons fresh lime juice

1. Place 3 cups water in large saucepan; bring to a boil over high heat. Add soup, shrimp, bell peppers, onions, salt and pepper.

2. Cook 3 to 5 minutes, stirring frequently, or until noodles are tender. Stir in lime juice. Serve immediately. *Makes 4 servings*

Homestyle Tuna Pot Pie

Line 9-inch pie pan with 1 pie crust dough round; set aside. Reserve second dough round. In medium bowl, combine remaining ingredients; mix well. Pour tuna mixture into pie shell; top with second crust. Crimp edges to seal. Cut slits in top crust to vent. Bake in 375°F oven 45 to 50 minutes or until golden brown.

Makes 6 servings

- 1 package (15 ounces) refrigerated pie crust dough
- 1 can (10¾ ounces) condensed cream of potato or cream of mushroom soup
- 1 package (10 ounces) frozen peas and carrots, thawed
- 1 (7-ounce) STARKIST Flavor Fresh Pouch® Tuna (Albacore or Chunk Light)
- ½ cup chopped onion
- ⅓ cup milk
- ½ teaspoon poultry seasoning or dried thyme leaves
- Salt and black pepper

Tuna and Broccoli Bake

1 package (16 ounces)
   frozen broccoli cuts,
   thawed and well
   drained
2 slices bread, cut in
   ½-inch cubes
1 (7-ounce) STARKIST
   Flavor Fresh Pouch®
   Tuna (Albacore or
   Chunk Light)
2 cups cottage cheese
1 cup shredded Cheddar
   cheese
3 eggs
¼ teaspoon ground black
   pepper

Place broccoli on bottom of 2-quart baking dish. Top with bread cubes and tuna. In medium bowl, combine cottage cheese, Cheddar cheese, eggs and pepper. Spread evenly over tuna mixture. Bake in 400°F oven 30 minutes or until golden brown and puffed.

Makes 4 servings

Creole Shrimp and Rice

1. Heat oil in large skillet over medium heat until hot. Add rice; cook and stir 2 to 3 minutes or until lightly browned.

2. Add tomatoes, water and seasoning blend; bring to a boil. Reduce heat; cover and simmer 15 minutes.

3. Add shrimp and okra. Cook, covered, 3 minutes or until heated through.

Makes 4 servings

Tip: Okra are oblong green pods. When cooked, they give off a viscous substance that acts as a good thickener.

2 tablespoons olive oil
1 cup uncooked white rice
1 can (about 14 ounces) diced tomatoes with garlic
1½ cups water
1 teaspoon Creole or Cajun seasoning blend
1 pound peeled cooked medium shrimp
1 package (10 ounces) frozen okra *or* 1½ cups frozen sugar snap peas, thawed

No-Fuss Fish

Salsa Shrimp and Rice

1 tablespoon olive oil
¼ cup chopped onion
1 clove garlic, minced
1 cup prepared green salsa
¾ cup white wine
1 tablespoon lemon juice
12 ounces medium raw
   shrimp, peeled
4 cups hot cooked rice

1. Heat large nonstick skillet over medium-high heat; add oil and heat until hot. Add onion; cook and stir until onion is translucent.

2. Add garlic; cook and stir 1 minute. Add salsa, wine and lemon juice; bring to a boil. Reduce heat to medium-low; simmer 10 minutes.

3. Add shrimp; cook about 2 minutes or until shrimp turn pink and opaque, stirring occasionally. Serve shrimp mixture over rice. *Makes 4 servings*

No-Fuss Fish

Tuna Noodle Casserole

Microwave Directions

Combine soup and milk in 2-quart microwavable shallow casserole. Stir in pasta, tuna, ⅔ *cup* French Fried Onions, vegetables and cheese. Cover; microwave on HIGH 10 minutes* or until heated through, stirring halfway through cooking time. Top with remaining ⅔ *cup* onions. Microwave 1 minute or until onions are golden.   *Makes 6 servings*

*Or bake, covered, in 350°F oven 25 to 30 minutes.

Tip: Garnish with chopped pimiento and parsley sprigs, if desired.

1 can (10¾ ounces)
   condensed cream of
   mushroom soup
1 cup milk
3 cups hot cooked rotini
   pasta (2 cups
   uncooked)
1 can (12½ ounces) tuna
   packed in water,
   drained and flaked
1⅓ cups *French's®* French
   Fried Onions, divided
1 package (10 ounces)
   frozen peas and
   carrots
½ cup (2 ounces) shredded
   Cheddar or grated
   Parmesan cheese

No-Fuss Fish

Speedy Sides

Scalloped Apples & Onions

1 medium onion, thinly
   sliced
4 tablespoons butter,
   melted, divided
5 red or green apples,
   cored and thinly sliced
8 ounces (1½ cups)
   pasteurized process
   cheese, cut into small
   pieces, divided
2 cups *French's®* French
   Fried Onions, divided

1. Preheat oven to 375°F. Sauté onion in 2 tablespoons butter in medium skillet over medium-high heat 3 minutes or until tender. Add apples and sauté 5 minutes or until apples are tender.

2. Stir 1 cup cheese, *1 cup* French Fried Onions and remaining melted butter into apple mixture. Transfer to greased 9-inch deep-dish pie plate.

3. Bake, uncovered, 20 minutes or until heated through. Top with remaining cheese and onions. Bake 5 minutes or until cheese is melted.

Makes 6 side-dish servings

Tip: To save time and cleanup, apple mixture may be baked in a heatproof skillet if desired. Wrap skillet handle in heavy-duty foil.

Variation: For added Cheddar flavor, substitute *French's®* **Cheddar French Fried Onions** for the original flavor.

Bowtie Zucchini

¼ cup vegetable oil
1 cup chopped onion
2 cloves garlic, minced
5 small zucchini, cut into thin strips
⅔ cup heavy cream
1 package (16 ounces) bowtie pasta, cooked and drained
3 tablespoons grated Parmesan cheese
Salt and black pepper

1. Preheat oven to 350°F.

2. Heat oil in large skillet over medium-high heat. Add onion and garlic; cook and stir until onion is tender. Add zucchini; cook and stir until tender.

3. Add cream; cook and stir until thickened. Add pasta and cheese to skillet. Season to taste with salt and pepper. Transfer mixture to 2-quart casserole. Cover and bake 15 minutes or until heated through. *Makes 8 servings*

Speedy Sides

Sesame Honey Vegetable Casserole

1. Preheat oven to 350°F. Place mixed vegetables in shallow 1½-quart casserole dish or quiche dish.

2. Combine honey, oil, soy sauce and sesame seeds; mix well. Drizzle evenly over vegetables. Bake 20 to 25 minutes or until vegetables are hot, stirring after 15 minutes. *Makes 4 side-dish servings*

1 package (16 ounces) frozen mixed vegetables such as baby carrots, broccoli, onions and red peppers, thawed and drained
3 tablespoons honey
1 tablespoon dark sesame oil
1 tablespoon soy sauce
2 teaspoons sesame seeds

Speedy Sides

Sombrero Vegetable Bake

1 tablespoon olive oil
1 clove garlic, minced
¼ teaspoon ground cumin
1 can (14½ ounces) stewed
    tomatoes
1 package (9 ounces)
    frozen corn, thawed
2 small zucchini, cut into
    ¾-inch chunks
2 tablespoons *Frank's®*
    RedHot® Original
    Cayenne Pepper Sauce
¼ teaspoon salt
1⅓ cups *French's®* French
    Fried Onions

Microwave Directions

Whisk together oil, garlic and cumin in 2-quart microwavable bowl. Microwave, uncovered, on HIGH 1 minute.

Stir in tomatoes with liquid, corn, zucchini, *Frank's RedHot* Sauce and salt. Cover tightly with plastic wrap. Microwave on HIGH 8 to 10 minutes or until zucchini is crisp-tender, stirring twice. Uncover; sprinkle with French Fried Onions. Microwave on HIGH 1 minute or until onions are golden.

Makes 6 side-dish servings

·146·

Speedy Sides

Potato Gorgonzola Gratin

Preheat oven to 400°F. In 8- or 9-inch square baking dish, arrange half the potatoes. Season generously with salt and pepper; sprinkle lightly with nutmeg. Top with onion and apple. Arrange remaining potatoes on top. Season again with salt and pepper; add milk. Cover dish with aluminum foil. Bake 30 to 40 minutes or until potatoes are tender. Remove foil; top with both cheeses. Bake, uncovered, 10 to 15 minutes or until top is lightly browned.   *Makes 4 to 6 servings*

Favorite recipe from **Colorado Potato Administrative Committee**

1 pound (2 medium-large)
   Colorado baking
   potatoes, unpeeled and
   very thinly sliced,
   divided
   Salt and black pepper
   Ground nutmeg
½ medium onion, thinly
   sliced
1 medium tart green apple,
   such as pippin or
   Granny Smith,
   unpeeled, cored and
   very thinly sliced
1 cup milk or half-and-half
¾ cup (3 ounces)
   Gorgonzola or other
   blue cheese, crumbled
2 tablespoons freshly
   grated Parmesan
   cheese

Creamy Vegetables & Pasta

1 can (10¾ ounces)
  condensed cream
  of chicken soup
1 cup milk
¼ cup grated Parmesan
  cheese
1 package (16 ounces)
  frozen seasoned pasta
  and vegetable
  combination
1⅓ cups *French's*® French
  Fried Onions, divided

Microwave Directions

Combine soup, milk and cheese in 2-quart microwavable shallow casserole. Stir in vegetable combination and ⅔ cup French Fried Onions. Microwave on HIGH 12 minutes* or until vegetables and pasta are crisp-tender, stirring halfway through cooking time. Sprinkle with remaining ⅔ cup onions. Microwave 1 minute or until onions are golden.   *Makes 6 servings*

Or, bake in preheated 350°F oven 30 to 35 minutes.

Tip: Add canned tuna or salmon for a great meatless dish. Serve with a salad on the side.

Speedy Sides

Green Beans with Blue Cheese and Roasted Peppers

1. Preheat oven to 350°F. Spray 2-quart oval casserole with nonstick cooking spray. Combine green beans, red pepper strips, salt and pepper in prepared dish.

2. Place cream cheese and milk in small saucepan; heat over low heat, stirring until melted. Add blue cheese; stir only until combined. Pour cheese mixture over green bean mixture. Stir until green beans are coated.

3. Combine bread crumbs and butter in small bowl; sprinkle evenly over casserole. Bake, uncovered, 20 minutes or until hot and bubbly.

Makes 4 servings

1 bag (20 ounces) frozen cut green beans
½ jar (about 3 ounces) roasted red pepper strips, drained and slivered
⅛ teaspoon salt
⅛ teaspoon white pepper
4 ounces cream cheese
½ cup milk
¾ cup blue cheese (3 ounces), crumbled
½ cup Italian-style bread crumbs
1 tablespoon butter, melted

Sweet Potatoes with Brandy and Raisins

½ cup seedless raisins
¼ cup brandy
4 medium sweet potatoes, boiled until just tender then peeled and sliced into ¼-inch slices
⅔ cup packed brown sugar
¼ cup FLEISCHMANN'S® Original Margarine
2 tablespoons water
¼ teaspoon ground cinnamon

1. Mix raisins and brandy in small bowl; let stand 20 minutes. Drain raisins.

2. Layer sweet potatoes in 9×9×2-inch baking pan; top with raisins.

3. Mix brown sugar, margarine, water and cinnamon in small saucepan; heat to a boil. Pour over sweet potatoes.

4. Bake in preheated 350°F oven for 40 minutes, basting with pan juices occasionally.

Makes 4 to 6 servings

Harvest Vegetable Scallop

Preheat oven to 375°F. In 12×8-inch baking dish, combine carrots, broccoli and ⅔ cup French Fried Onions. Tuck potato slices into vegetable mixture at an angle. Dot vegetables evenly with cheese spread. Pour milk over vegetables; sprinkle with seasonings as desired. Bake, covered, 30 minutes or until vegetables are tender. Top with remaining ⅔ cup onions; bake, uncovered, 3 minutes or until onions are golden brown.

Makes 6 servings

Microwave Directions: In 12×8-inch microwavable dish, prepare vegetables as above. Top with cheese spread, milk and seasonings as above. Cook, covered, on HIGH 12 to 14 minutes or until vegetables are tender, rotating dish halfway through cooking time. Top with remaining onions; cook, uncovered, 1 minute. Let stand 5 minutes.

4 medium carrots, thinly sliced
1 package (10 ounces) frozen chopped broccoli, thawed and drained
1⅓ cups *French's*® French Fried Onions, divided
5 small red potatoes, sliced ⅛ inch thick
1 jar (8 ounces) pasteurized processed cheese spread
¼ cup milk
Freshly ground black pepper
Seasoned salt

Speedy Sides

Baked Tomato Risotto

1 jar (28 ounces) pasta
    sauce
1 can (14 ounces) chicken
    broth
2 cups sliced zucchini
1 cup arborio rice
1 can (4 ounces) sliced
    mushrooms, drained
2 cups (8 ounces) shredded
    mozzarella cheese

1. Preheat oven to 350°F. Spray 3-quart casserole with nonstick cooking spray.

2. Combine pasta sauce, broth, zucchini, rice and mushrooms in prepared dish.

3. Bake, covered, 30 minutes. Remove from oven; stir casserole. Cover; bake 15 to 20 minutes or until rice is tender. Remove from oven; sprinkle evenly with cheese. Bake, uncovered, 5 minutes or until cheese is melted.

Makes 6 servings

Apple & Carrot Casserole

1. Preheat oven to 350°F. Cook carrots in boiling water in large saucepan 5 minutes; drain. Layer carrots and apples in large casserole.

2. Combine flour, brown sugar and nutmeg in small bowl; sprinkle over top. Dot with butter; pour orange juice over flour mixture. Sprinkle with salt. Bake 30 minutes or until carrots are tender. *Makes 6 servings*

6 large carrots, sliced
4 large apples, peeled, quartered, cored and sliced
¼ cup plus 1 tablespoon all-purpose flour
1 tablespoon packed brown sugar
½ teaspoon ground nutmeg
1 tablespoon butter
½ cup orange juice
½ teaspoon salt

Acknowledgments

The publisher would like to thank the companies and organizations listed below for the use of their recipes and photographs in this publication.

Birds Eye Foods

Bob Evans®

Colorado Potato Administrative Committee

Del Monte Corporation

Fleischmann's® Margarines and Spreads

The Golden Grain Company®

The Hidden Valley® Food Products Company

Hillshire Farm®

Lawry's® Foods

MASTERFOODS USA

National Turkey Federation

North Dakota Beef Commission

Reckitt Benckiser Inc.

Riviana Foods Inc.

Sargento® Foods Inc.

StarKist Seafood Company

Unilever Foods North America

Veg•All®

Index

METRIC CONVERSION CHART

VOLUME MEASUREMENTS (dry)

1/8 teaspoon = 0.5 mL
1/4 teaspoon = 1 mL
1/2 teaspoon = 2 mL
3/4 teaspoon = 4 mL
1 teaspoon = 5 mL
1 tablespoon = 15 mL
2 tablespoons = 30 mL
1/4 cup = 60 mL
1/3 cup = 75 mL
1/2 cup = 125 mL
2/3 cup = 150 mL
3/4 cup = 175 mL
1 cup = 250 mL
2 cups = 1 pint = 500 mL
3 cups = 750 mL
4 cups = 1 quart = 1 L

VOLUME MEASUREMENTS (fluid)

1 fluid ounce (2 tablespoons) = 30 mL
4 fluid ounces (1/2 cup) = 125 mL
8 fluid ounces (1 cup) = 250 mL
12 fluid ounces (1 1/2 cups) = 375 mL
16 fluid ounces (2 cups) = 500 mL

WEIGHTS (mass)

1/2 ounce = 15 g
1 ounce = 30 g
3 ounces = 90 g
4 ounces = 120 g
8 ounces = 225 g
10 ounces = 285 g
12 ounces = 360 g
16 ounces = 1 pound = 450 g

DIMENSIONS

1/16 inch = 2 mm
1/8 inch = 3 mm
1/4 inch = 6 mm
1/2 inch = 1.5 cm
3/4 inch = 2 cm
1 inch = 2.5 cm

OVEN TEMPERATURES

250°F = 120°C
275°F = 140°C
300°F = 150°C
325°F = 160°C
350°F = 180°C
375°F = 190°C
400°F = 200°C
425°F = 220°C
450°F = 230°C

BAKING PAN SIZES

Utensil	Size in Inches/Quarts	Metric Volume	Size in Centimeters
Baking or Cake Pan (square or rectangular)	8×8×2	2 L	20×20×5
	9×9×2	2.5 L	23×23×5
	12×8×2	3 L	30×20×5
	13×9×2	3.5 L	33×23×5
Loaf Pan	8×4×3	1.5 L	20×10×7
	9×5×3	2 L	23×13×7
Round Layer Cake Pan	8×1½	1.2 L	20×4
	9×1½	1.5 L	23×4
Pie Plate	8×1¼	750 mL	20×3
	9×1¼	1 L	23×3
Baking Dish or Casserole	1 quart	1 L	—
	1½ quart	1.5 L	—
	2 quart	2 L	—